TEACHING ADULT ENGLISH LANGUAGE LEARNERS

The Professional Practices in Adult Education and Lifelong Learning Series explores issues and concerns of practitioners who work in the broad range of settings in adult and continuing education and lifelong learning.

The books provide information and strategies on how to make practice more effective for professionals and those they serve. They are written from a practical viewpoint and provide a forum for instructors, administrators, policy makers, counselors, trainers, instructional designers, and other related professionals. The series contains single author or coauthored books only and does not include edited volumes.

Sharan B. Merriam
Ronald M. Cervero
Series Editors

TEACHING ADULT ENGLISH LANGUAGE LEARNERS

Richard A. Orem

KRIEGER PUBLISHING COMPANY
MALABAR, FLORIDA
2005

Original Edition 2005

Printed and Published by
KRIEGER PUBLISHING COMPANY
KRIEGER DRIVE
MALABAR, FLORIDA 32950

FROM A DECLARATION OF PRINCIPLES JOINTLY ADOPTED BY A COM-
MITTEE OF THE AMERICAN BAR ASSOCIATION AND A COMMITTEE OF
PUBLISHERS:

This publication is designed to provide accurate and authoritative information in
regard to the subject matter covered. It is sold with the understanding that the
publisher is not engaged in rendering legal, accounting, or other professional service.
If legal advice or other expert assistance is required, the services of a competent
professional person should be sought.

Library of Congress Cataloging-in-Publication Data

Orem, Richard A.
    Teaching adult English language learners / Richard A. Orem.
       p.   cm. — (Professional practices in adult education and lifelong
       learning series)
    Includes bibliographical references (p.) and index.
    ISBN 1-57524-219-2 (alk. paper)
       1. English language—Study and teaching—Foreign speakers. 2. Adult
education. I. Title. II. Series.

PE1128.A2O75 2005
428'.0071'5—dc22   2004063359

10   9   8   7   6   5   4   3   2

CONTENTS

PREFACE

When I started teaching adult English language learners in 1969, the profession of teaching English as a second or foreign language was in its infancy. TESOL (Teachers of English to Speakers of Other Languages), the professional organization, had just formed three years earlier. English was gaining currency as the major world language in the 1960s, largely due to the expanding world diplomatic and military presence of the United States, the establishment of the Peace Corps with its emphasis on English language education in developing countries, and the spread of British and American pop culture. In the United States, teachers of English to new English language learners were found mainly in large urban centers and gateways of immigrants, including Chicago, Los Angeles, San Francisco, Miami, New York, and Washington, DC. Bilingual education was beginning to receive official sanction thanks to various court decisions and laws resulting from the wave of social justice-oriented legislation emerging from the civil rights movement.

Now the practice of teaching English to speakers of other languages is supported by a growing body of research literature and a vibrant international professional community led by TESOL, together with many national, state, and regional affiliates. In the United States, language diversity has become not just a "problem" of urban education, but is a hallmark of public education throughout the country. In many states, among programs funded by the federal government for adult learners with less than a high school education, the population of adult English language learners served by these programs outnumbers adult learners whose first language is English and who are learning basic literacy.

Serving these adult English language learners with qualified instructors is a major problem for many providers. Part-time teachers, most of whom have had little or no training in teaching English as a second language (ESL), fill the overwhelming majority of teaching positions in these programs. The number of undergraduate and graduate programs in U.S. colleges and universities designed to prepare teachers of English language learners has increased consistently over the past two decades, but most graduates of these programs will eventually work in elementary or secondary schools, or work in other countries. Relatively few will make a career of teaching adult English language learners.

Staff development, therefore, becomes an ongoing need. The purpose of this book is to provide program administrators and teachers with insights into the teaching of adult English language learners as experienced by an adult educator whose career in the field stretches over 35 years. These insights are gleaned from actual experience of teaching and teacher training, both in and outside the United States.

Chapter 1 begins by defining terms and asking a number of important questions as a way of establishing a context for later chapters. Who are adult English language learners? Who does and does not participate in adult ESL programs? What are programs for adult English language learners? What do we know about how adults learn? What do we know about how adults acquire another language? What are some common principles that support effective instruction? What is your personal philosophy of teaching and why is it important to be able to articulate a personal philosophy?

Chapter 2 focuses on a central element for most adult English language teaching. How do you teach oral skills (speaking and listening)? This question is answered by providing three scenarios demonstrating major characteristics of approaches widely used over the years to teach listening and speaking to adult English language learners. These scenarios mark various stages of development of my work in the field. They are examined in relation to the TESOL organization's standards for instruction in adult ESL programs.

Chapter 3 continues this discussion of classroom practice by focusing on the teaching of literacy skills (reading and writing). Three major movements characterize significant influences on the teaching of literacy to adult English language learners. The first movement came to be known as competency-based adult education. The second movement is known for its political orientation and participant involvement. Participatory adult literacy emerged following the early writings of Paulo Freire, a Brazilian adult educator, and came to be adopted by some largely urban, community-based programs in the United States. The third movement, designed primarily for teaching reading and writing, is also known as whole language. Within whole language, the language experience approach represents an effective technique for teaching basic literacy to adult English language learners. The cloze procedure is also discussed as an effective tool for determining appropriate readability or assessing comprehension. Finally, the chapter provides suggestions for effectively teaching writing that reflect assumptions of communicative language teaching.

Chapter 4, Organizing Instruction, shifts attention from teaching practice to program planning. The focus is on comparing traditional and nontraditional curriculum development approaches found in many adult education programs for English language learners. In this chapter, the primary nontraditional approach to curriculum development is the participatory approach, a basically learner-centered approach that relies on collaboration of teacher and learners, and use of authentic materials derived from the learner's own lived experiences.

Chapter 5, Teaching Cross-Cultural Skills, focuses on developing practical knowledge of how culture affects the teaching-learning transaction. It draws from the research of the Dutch anthropologist Geert Hofstede to show how teachers and learners bring different worldviews to the classroom, views that may seriously impact the effectiveness of instruction. An awareness of these differences can prepare the adult educator for some of the inevitable problems that will arise in the classroom. The chapter includes a number of other activities and resources that could enhance teachers' and administrators' awareness of the role of culture in the adult English language learning classroom. Among the suggested activities are the reflective essay, the cultural field trip, journal writing, critical incidents, open discussion, values clarification, and simulation exercises. Among suggested resources are a number of videos that I have found effective with teachers and administrators as part of an ongoing staff development program.

Finally, Chapter 6 is a look at the future of the profession of adult English language teaching. Recent efforts to develop a research agenda for adult ESL reveal the belief that the field at large needs to better understand the language learning and teaching processes. The standards movement is already impacting the education of children. With the reauthorization of the federal legislation funding adult education, we will likely see a greater emphasis on accountability in adult ESL programs. The most likely outcome of this emphasis on accountability will be the development of standards that will affect the content of instruction and the assessment of learning outcomes in adult education. Given what has happened in elementary and secondary education, this new emphasis on standards will place new burdens on administrators of adult education programs, and reinforce the need for programs to employ a greater percentage of full-time staff who can devote time to curriculum and staff development.

ACKNOWLEDGMENTS

I have had the benefit of many mentors in my career in adult ESL. My successes as a teacher educator and adult educator are due in large measure to the guidance I have received from individuals I respect a great deal. Among those mentors I include John Haskell and Jean Handscombe, both of whom opened doors for my greater involvement within the profession when I was new in the field. Closer to home, this book would not be possible without the inspiration of my wife, Sue, who initially opened my eyes to the profession of adult education. She embodies the most essential qualities of effective teaching that I have come to associate with ESL teachers who unselfishly devote their time and talents to helping English language learners succeed against all odds.

THE AUTHOR

Richard Orem is professor of literacy education and adult and higher education at Northern Illinois University in DeKalb, Illinois. His first contact with the field of teaching English as a second or foreign language occurred in 1969 with an invitation to the Peace Corps. In 1973, following a one-year tour as a Teacher Corps intern in the Atlanta Public Schools, and two years at the Bourguiba Institute in Tunis, Tunisia, he completed his master's degree in language education at the University of Georgia, taught high school English for two years in Atlanta, then returned to the University of Georgia to complete a doctorate in adult education in 1977. During this time he also taught adult ESL and consulted with the State of Georgia to deliver adult ESL instruction to the growing refugee population moving to that state after 1975.

Orem arrived at Northern Illinois University in 1978 to find a vibrant statewide community of adult educators active in the teaching of English as a second language (ESL). He became involved with Illinois TESOL/BE (Teachers of English to Speakers of Other Languages/Bilingual Education), serving as that affiliate's president and executive secretary for six consecutive years. He was elected to the executive board of TESOL in 1988 and chaired TESOL 89 in San Antonio, Texas; in 1989–90, he spent the year as executive director of TESOL in Alexandria, Virginia.

Since 1990, Orem has continued to be active in adult education, K-12 teacher education, and TESOL-related professional activities, and has consulted with a variety of state agencies and international programs in Europe and Asia. At Northern Illinois

University, in addition to teaching, he is university advisor for ESL and bilingual teacher certification and is co-director of a Title III professional development grant from the Department of Education.

CHAPTER 1

Getting Started

I remember reporting to Peace Corps training at the University of Utah in June 1969 with 99 other young men. Everyone had his own story to share about what brought him to this program. This was a male-only training program because we were about to enter a highly segregated society. Fifty married couples and a few single women were training in a small border community in southern Arizona. They would be assigned to the more "cosmopolitan" cities of Tripoli and Benghazi. The men? We were bound for the oasis villages of the deep desert province of the Fezzan. It would be years later before I would realize that this would not be an unusual story shared by English language teachers around the world. It would also be years later before I realized that I was about to begin a personal career journey that summer. And I was not going to look back.

My own career journey started long before I realized I even had a career. You could say it started officially with my invitation to a Peace Corps training program in the summer of 1969. Before that training program had ended, I became a "victim" of a military coup in the Kingdom of Libya. On September 1, a young Libyan army lieutenant by the name of Moammar Ghaddafi led a coup that overthrew the aging King Idris. Several weeks later the Peace Corps withdrew from Libya, leaving several hundred volunteers without a program. Fortunately, some of us ended up in another training program that would eventually take us to Tunisia, Libya's next door neighbor. There we became the English faculty of the Bourguiba Institute, a modern language school affiliated with the University of Tunis.

I eventually returned to the States after my tour in Tunisia where I would complete a graduate degree, teach in an inner city school in Atlanta, then return to the University of Georgia to enroll in a doctoral program in adult education. My interest had shifted in those three years since returning from Tunisia, from returning to the Middle East to teach English as a foreign language, to staying in the States to work in literacy. But I never strayed far from an involvement with teaching English as a second language. World events wouldn't let me. The Vietnam conflict had ended in 1975 and the United States was experiencing a tidal wave of refugees from Southeast Asia. Government policy would attempt to resettle these refugees in isolated communities to avoid a reghettoization of urban America. Several families landed in Northeast Georgia and I was called upon to offer some assistance to the schools where the children would enroll, and to teach the adult members of the families. I can still remember the expressions on their faces. They truly looked displaced.

This is the start of my story as an adult ESL teacher. Others have their own stories to share that relate how they came to teach adult ESL. For me, that was over 30 years ago. In the United States of 2004, if I were to paint the adult ESL teacher population in broad-brush strokes, I would paint it overwhelmingly white, middle class, and female. What is also characteristic of these adult ESL teachers is that they have limited, if any, training. Meanwhile, they are teaching English to a more diverse immigrant population than ever before.

DEFINING TERMS

Before I begin, I need to explain the use of several terms throughout this text. For the major part of my career in this field, English as a second language (ESL) was the term commonly used to describe the learner and the programs that taught these learners. Other terms are commonly found in the literature and serve only to confuse the layperson. These terms include ESL, EFL, TESL, TESOL, and TEAL. Use of these terms varies according to whether you are speaking of English as a second language (ESL), English as a foreign language (EFL), the act or academic degree of teaching English as a second language (TESL), the professional organization of Teachers of English to Speakers of Other Languages (TESOL), or the term used commonly in Canada, teaching English as an additional language (TEAL).

Fairly recently a new phrase has entered the discourse, English language learner. This phrase is less restrictive in that many of the students learning English are learning it as a third or fourth language. This new phrase is appearing more frequently in the literature and in government documents. Therefore, I am going to use it especially when referring to students. I will continue to use ESL (or adult ESL) when referring to programs, or when specific literature uses that term (such as the TESOL publication, *Standards for Adult Education ESL Programs*).

WHO ARE ADULT ENGLISH LANGUAGE LEARNERS?

Diversity is a word that is often repeated in discussions of education and workforce preparation. The 2000 Census led some commentators to report that "never have we been so diverse" (Prewitt, 2002, p. 6). More recent analyses of 2000 census data have determined that Hispanics now outnumber African-Americans as the largest minority group in the United States. But the growth of the U.S. population is not due just to Hispanics. The major sources of population growth in the United States are immigrants in general, especially those populations with the highest immigration and birth rates (primarily Latino from Central and South America). The numbers of foreign-born, non-native English speakers in the United States, as a percentage of the total population, are at the highest levels they have been in more than a century. This implies that the demand for English language training will continue to increase well into the 21st century. A strong indicator of this growth within the English language learning population can be seen in the dramatic surge just within the K-12 student population. From the 1989–1990 academic year to the 1999–2000 academic year, the reported number of English language learners enrolled in Pre-Kindergarten through Grade 12 more than doubled nationwide, representing the largest growth of any demographic segment of the U.S. school population (Kindler, 2002). These trends are continuing into the current decade.

Likewise, the growth in numbers of adult English language learners has been increasing dramatically, and now outnumbers adult students enrolled in programs of adult basic education in many states. This growth can also be seen in the volunteer sector. Over 75% of Laubach Literacy member programs provide ESL instruction. Nearly half (45%) of all students received ESL instruction in 2000, up from 31% in 1995 (Laubach Literacy Action, 2001).

Even beyond the borders of the United States, adult English language learners can be found anywhere and everywhere in the world. Since World War II, the dominance of the United States as a world power has meant more than military and economic dominance. It has also meant cultural dominance. Never in the history of the world has one language come to dominate global communication. In part thanks to British colonialism from the early 18th through the mid 20th centuries, and the popularity of American pop culture through the 20th and into the 21st centuries, English is now spoken by more people than any other language in the history of the world, and is spoken by more people as a percentage of the total world population than at any previous time in recorded history. English is the language of international transportation and commerce. English is the dominant language of computers and mass media. When students protest American foreign policy in Jakarta or Tehran or Seoul, CNN televises their signs written in English.

In the United States, adult English language learners are found among our growing numbers of immigrants and refugees who are seeking escape from war, famine, and economic hardship, and who continue to see the United States as their last chance. Many of these immigrants and refugees also are seeking a chance for themselves and their children to gain access to education, to job skills, and to a more positive economic future.

English language learners can also be found among the growing number of highly trained professionals from countries around the world where opportunities for employment are unavailable or denied, where access to higher and continuing education is denied or nonexistent. Institutions of higher education in the United States continue to attract thousands of the most highly educated people of the developing countries of the world. They often bring spouses and children who enter our educational system at elementary, secondary, and postsecondary levels. Those no longer eligible for secondary education are served by federally funded programs in community colleges and community-based organizations. In many cases, employers provide English language instruction in order to ensure a safer and more loyal workforce.

Adult English language learners can be 16 to 60 years old or older, but most tend to be in their 20s. They may be professionally trained immigrants from Russia, or they may be illiterate refugees from Somalia. They may have landed yesterday at O'Hare Airport or they may have lived their entire lives in the United States. They may already know enough English to ask very sophisticated questions about the grammar of the language, or they may want simply to learn how to communicate orally with their work supervisor.

WHO DOES AND DOES NOT PARTICIPATE IN ADULT ESL PROGRAMS?

Ever since the federal government has been funding adult ESL programs, we have had a good idea of who participates in these programs. We also have a good idea of who doesn't participate. In fact, characteristics of participants and nonparticipants in adult ESL programs have been very consistent over many decades of data collection. Participants tend to be young, with higher levels of formal schooling in their first language, and relatively new in the country (National Center for Education Statistics, 1998). Nonparticipants tend to be those with lower levels of formal schooling in their first language and for that reason are the hardest to reach and teach (Valentine, 1990). And because of the demands placed on programs by federal law, these nonparticipants are not actively sought because they tend to show the poorest results in terms of demonstrating program success. Unfortunately, estimates of participation and nonparticipation rates in adult ESL programs have been at best unreliable because of the highly transient nature of a large portion of this target population.

Those who don't participate in adult ESL classes often report that they weren't aware of programs. And when they do know about the programs, they identify such barriers as time, cost, and childcare or transportation as those factors that prevent their participation. In order to overcome these barriers, local programs have gone to great lengths to reach out to nonparticipants through various media, through word of mouth campaigns, through faith-based and community organizations, and more. Some programs have provided childcare on the premises. In fact, childcare has traditionally been one of the most persistent barriers to participation in adult education programs. Family literacy programs attempt to eliminate that barrier when preschool-age children are involved by actually focusing instruction on the interaction of parents and their children. Likewise, transportation is a frequently cited barrier. This has led many programs to establish satellite centers where the target population lives, or they provide transportation to instructional centers.

Then there are those adult learners who don't participate because they don't see the relevance of the program to their lives. These nonparticipants have been called resisters and their numbers are significant (Quigley, 1997). Programs can't simply offer classes and expect adults to attend. The programs need to make sure the curriculum meets the needs of the learners and offers them language that will be useful, that will empower them.

WHAT ARE PROGRAMS FOR ENGLISH LANGUAGE LEARNERS?

Programs for English language learners come in many different sizes and flavors, depending on funding source, program context, and student goals. For nearly 50 years, the primary funding source for adult ESL programs has been the federal government. In the 1960s, the federal government began to fund basic literacy programs as part of the Great Society legislation. Initially these programs were designed to provide native English speaking adults a second chance to learn to read and write and to eventually earn a high school diploma. Provision was included to offer English language instruction to those for whom English was not their home, or first, language. These initial programs focused on conversation as well as reading and writing. Sophisticated levels of literacy were not the goal for many students in these programs. Rather, they were interested in general "survival" skills. There were still plenty of jobs in the manufacturing industrial sector that did not require advanced literacy skill.

As we enter the 21st century, conditions have dramatically changed. Legislation for adult education has gone through many revisions. The current legislation is named the Adult Education and Family Literacy Act (AEFLA), Title II of the Workforce Investment Act of 1998 (P.L. 105-220). Its very name conveys the emphasis of the federal government's interest in this legislation. Adult education programs, including adult ESL programs, prepare adults for the workforce (Stein, 2000). Instruction has become more sophisticated as the need for advanced workskills becomes a standard expectation. Furthermore, current legislation supports efforts at citizenship education (Tolbert, 2001).

Programs for English language learners continue to provide instruction in social survival skills, but they must also, by law, provide instruction in work-related language (Marshall, 2002). Providers of English language instruction vary from state to state and community to community. In some states, the primary providers are the system of community colleges or vocational technical schools that are designed for adult learners. In some states, the primary providers are the public schools whose mission is to serve the adult population still lacking a high school diploma or equivalent. In some urban areas, important providers are community-based or other private organizations that are organized to meet the needs of particular community groups, while elsewhere churches or other faith-based organizations provide programs of English language instruction, often primarily with volunteer tutors. In some areas, employers have assumed a greater responsibility for basic skills training, including English language skills for non-native English speakers. These programs tend to focus on specific work-related language.

Some programs are organized around family structures. Family literacy is now a widely recognized form of program structure in which parents and small children come together at the same time and in the same place for learning (Weinstein-Shr & Quintero, 1995). Curricula are developed to provide children the necessary readiness skills they need in elementary schools, while at the same time parents are instructed in literacy and parenting so they can be more helpful to their children.

WHAT DO WE KNOW ABOUT HOW ADULTS LEARN?

Along with the growth in programs for adult learners has come increased understanding of how adults learn. Some of the principles of adult learning that have received widespread acceptance for their relevance to general adult education program planning have also been widely accepted for their specific application to developing programs for adult English language learners.

One of the most widely recognized names in adult education in the United States is Malcolm Knowles. His principles of adult learning, commonly known as andragogy (Knowles, 1980, 1984), have been used for nearly 40 years by adult educators in various program settings. What are these principles and how do they apply to adult English language learners?

First, adult learners become more self-directed as they mature. According to Knowles, younger learners are more dependent on others to guide their learning processes. This is not to say that younger learners do not also exhibit on occasion a degree of self-direction, of initiating their own learning, of showing a basic curiosity for learning. However, curricula designed for younger learners have more often than not assumed that teachers or other authorities need to establish the content of learning. Effective adult education programs should recognize the need for adult learners to set their own goals. Another fact is that effective adult education recognizes the voluntary nature of adult learning. This principle also recognizes the nonformal and informal nature of so much of adult learning that takes place worldwide.

Second, adults learn best when new learning is related to past experiences. We can all relate to this principle if we think of the last time we were in a classroom in the role of the learner. How did we feel if the instructor did not take the time to assess where we were before trying to teach? How did we feel if we thought the instructor was not willing to recognize that we all come to the classroom with a different set of experiences? Knowles's second principle stresses that adult learning can be facilitated more effectively when we validate the learners' previous experiences. Adult English language learners bring a rich experience base to the classroom as well. It becomes the responsibility of the effective teacher to validate that life experience in the curriculum.

Third, adults learn best when they are ready to learn, when they feel a need to know or do something in their role as parent, worker, or community member, for example. Adult English language learners have an immediate need to learn to communicate in these various roles, so readiness to learn is not an issue. Likewise, once they have learned to communicate to effectively perform a specific role, they may feel they no longer need to return to class. This intermittent attendance becomes a source of frustration for programs that depend on steady attendance and achievement toward predetermined goals as justification for funding.

Fourth, adults learn more effectively if their learning is organized around problems they face in their daily lives, rather than subject matter that is determined by someone else. Knowles refers to this as orientation to learning. Educational curricula for children and adolescents have been traditionally organized around content areas. High school graduation requirements specify so many units of science, math, social studies, and language arts. Many younger learners fail to see the relevance in studying algebra or world history, especially when these subjects are not made relevant to their more immediate life experiences. Effective adult education instruction is problem-based, attempting to gear teaching to help adults find solutions to the problems they face in their immediate life experience. Adult English language learners are faced with many problems in their everyday lives. Problem-based curricula reflect this third principle.

Finally, adult learners have a desire to learn. All adults learn, but at different rates and in different ways. Some feel they cannot learn in a formal institutional setting such as a school, maybe because they experienced failure in school as a child. Adults who have been successful in formal programs tend to do better in those same settings. Those who have not experienced success tend to have lower self-esteem and less confidence in their own abilities. Therefore, it is important for any adult educator to recognize the innate desire of all adults to learn and to provide positive reinforcement of their accomplishments, no matter how small.

One of my favorite adult educators, who comes to the subject of adult learning from a culturally diverse background, is Jane Vella. Her 1994 book entitled *Learning to Listen, Learning to Teach: The Power of Dialogue in Educating Adults,* although written for a more general audience of adult educators, speaks eloquently to the very issues that so many adult English language learners bring with them to the classroom.

Vella's central assumption in this discussion is that "adult learning is best achieved in dialogue" (p. 3). The 12 principles of adult learning she provides are all designed "to begin and maintain and nurture the dialogue" (p. 3). I believe that many adult educators who have been exposed to the writings of Knowles and Freire would agree. But do they apply this principle in their everyday practice?

Vella's principle 1 is needs assessment. This principle requires the adult educator to acknowledge that learners come from a variety of backgrounds and have different goals for what they want to take away from class. Principle 2 is safety and speaks to the necessity for establishing an environment in which the learner has confidence in the learning process. Vella's principle 3, sound relationships, requires that the relationship between teacher and learner is built upon mutual respect. Principle 4, sequence and reinforcement, speaks to the need for logical organization and repetition of key concepts.

Principle 5 is praxis, a concept taken from the original writings of Freire. Vella writes that praxis is "doing with built-in reflection" (p. 11), and as a process is ongoing in our daily lived experiences. Principle 6 is respect for learners, recognizing that adults want to be the subjects of their own learning, not the objects. Principle 7 recognizes the need to teach to the different learning styles of your students, "learning with the mind, emotions, and muscles." (p. 14). Vella's principle 8 is labeled immediacy and reflects what Knowles talks about in his theory of andragogy as relevance.

Principle 9 can be an especially difficult principle to adhere to for both student and teacher. Vella defines this principle as "recognition of the impact of clear roles in the communication between learner and teacher" (p. 17). She draws an example from a conversation she had with Paulo Freire in which Freire said, "Only the student can name the moment of the death of the professor" (p. 17). Vella is telling us that so long as there is a power gap between teacher and student, learning will not take place effectively. The learner and teacher must see themselves as collaborators in the process of problem solving. Given the power gaps that exist within certain cultures (Hosfstede, 1980), it is no wonder that some students have a difficult time warming up to the idea of teacher and student as co-learners. This leads to principle 10, teamwork, which also assumes the presence of other principles, such as safety and needs assessment. We hear often about how teams are used successfully in different contexts, but do we honor this principle in our teaching? Principle 11, engagement, is illustrated with the metaphor of "jumping into the deep water" (p. 21). Learners who are engaged will experience a much deeper level of learning.

And finally, principle 12, accountability, "one of the foremost principles of adult learning" (p. 21). Educators are confronted daily with the demands of accountability. Here Vella admonishes adult educators to be accountable to the learner. Accountability is the last principle because it subsumes the implementation of all of the previous principles, honoring the contract between teacher and learner.

WHAT DO WE KNOW ABOUT HOW ADULTS ACQUIRE ANOTHER LANGUAGE?

At the time I entered the field of adult ESL in the early 1970s very little was known about how adults learn a second language. The research base was only beginning to develop. Thirty years later we have some well-developed theories of adult second language acquisition based primarily on observation of children and college-educated adults (Brown, 2000; Krashen, 1982; Larsen-Freeman & Long, 1991). However, we still don't have all the answers. What we do know can be boiled down to some useful propositions that guide my own teaching:

1. Language must be meaningful. Effective language instruction is that which incorporates language that is immediately useful for the learner.

2. Adults learn language that is comprehensible. Effective language instruction is that which introduces vocabulary and structures within contexts that help the learner understand meaning. Lack of comprehension will quickly discourage the adult learner from learning English.

3. Adults learn best when they feel safe to make mistakes. Effective language instruction provides a safe environment in which the learner feels secure and free from embarrassment. Some cultures speak of "saving face." The adult educator needs to avoid causing the learner to lose face.

4. Adults often experience a silent period early in the language learning process. Effective language instruction recognizes that some learners are not going to want to say anything for a while. But the instructor should not assume that, just be-

cause the learner is silent, the learner is not learning. For some learners this silent period will last longer than for others.

5. Adults learn at widely varying rates and through different modalities. Effective language instruction acknowledges the differences in learning rates among different learners. Some learners will make much faster progress than others. We do know that learners who have attained higher levels of formal schooling in their first language will tend to make faster progress toward acquiring a second language (Thomas & Collier, 2002). Different learners tend to rely on different learning modalities. A learner who relies on oral language will probably make faster progress in a classroom based on an oral approach. A learner who relies on visual learning will probably make faster progress in a classroom based on visual input, including written language and visual representations of language concepts.

Recently, the concept of social identity has been receiving a lot of attention by second language acquisition researchers (McKay & Wong, 1996; Peirce, 1995). Peirce (1995) talks about "investment in the target language" as a way to describe the more complex relationship between the learner and the social world of that learner. This requires a discussion of power relationships between the language learner and those with whom the learner wishes to communicate (Ullman, 1997). Power is discussed as it relates to race, sex, and class, and can offer a more robust explanation to the language learner as to why simply learning the second language (L2) is not sufficient for achieving a better job, better education for their children, a stable family structure, good health care, and more.

WHAT ARE SOME COMMON PRINCIPLES THAT SUPPORT EFFECTIVE INSTRUCTION?

Based, therefore, on what we know in general about how adults learn and how they learn a second language, we can say the following about what we know about effective instructional strategies for the adult ESL classroom:

1. Know your students. Be aware of their lived experiences. Not only relate their life experience to the new language they are learning, but acknowledge that problems in language learning can be traced to problems in their everyday lives, with jobs, family, health, and more.

2. Present language in different formats. Adults learn more effectively when they can see the language, hear the language, and manipulate the language.

3. Foster a safe learning environment. Adults can be readily intimidated in the second language classroom, especially if they have not had successful learning experiences in formal classrooms before. Encourage initiative. Be positive.

4. Use authentic materials. Adults want to learn language that is relevant. This means not only relating the language to their life experience, but also using language in formats that are useful. If your adult learner needs to learn language found at work, provide them with work-related vocabulary and structures.

5. Provide constructive feedback. Adults usually want to know how they are doing. Do not ignore their desire for feedback. At the same time, refrain from excessive feedback that may come across as insincere.

WHAT IS YOUR PERSONAL PHILOSOPHY OF TEACHING?

I want to end this chapter with a discussion of personal philosophy and its role in teaching adult ESL. Reflection has become a key component of continuing professional development and conventional teacher education. Recent publications (Casanave & Schecter, 1997; Freeman & Richards, 1996; Gebhard & Oprandy, 1999; Johnson & Golombek, 2002) encourage language educators to reflect on the role of developing and applying a personal belief system. Unfortunately, because of the part-time nature of the field, few adult educators reach this level of self-reflection.

Reflection is incorporated into our professional standards (National Board for Professional Teaching Standards, 1998; TESOL, 2003). I build reflective activities into my graduate courses. A typical response to these assignments is first resistance (This is so hard!), then gratitude (This was the best assignment!). These assignments make my own graduate students uncomfortable because they have never had to think about their own assumptions before. What do you believe about teaching adults? What do you believe about how adults learn English as a second language?

But whether you are a graduate student or a practicing teacher or program administrator, these questions force us to go beyond simply repeating words found in a textbook. To answer them honestly, we need to reflect on our own actions as educators. What has worked and what hasn't worked? What did we do to alter our practice to enable our students to become successful learners? In effect, one outcome of writing this book has been my own further development as a teacher educator.

My experiences of second language learning, followed by second language teaching and second language teacher education, span more than 40 years. During this time I have been directly associated with many different methods. I have worked in several different countries as well as the United States. I have worked with adults who are professionally educated and have tried to teach adults who lack even a basic elementary education. Reflecting on this, the greatest personal rewards come from hearing of the successes of those adult English language learners who have started their personal language learning journeys at the most basic levels and who succeed in achieving their life goals in the face of tremendous challenges. In the remaining chapters I will share insights gained from my experiences in preparing adult educators to teach adult English language learners. I find it a wonderful journey!

SUMMARY

This chapter introduces some basic definitions of terms commonly used in the field of practice. Following these definitions is a discussion of who adult English language learners are and who participants tend to be in adult ESL programs. Next is a description of basic principles of adult learning and the relevance of these principles to adult second language learners, followed by a discussion of how knowledge of these principles can lead to assumptions that underlie effective instruction in adult ESL programs. The chapter emphasizes the development of a personal philosophy of teaching adult English language learners. It is important as teachers and administrators in the field that you spend time reflecting on your practice. What works and what doesn't work?

The next several chapters will focus our attention on the specifics of instruction. I will share with you what I have learned about teaching oral skills, teaching literacy skills, developing programs, and emphasizing the role of cross-cultural understanding in developing a more complete rapport with adult English language learners.

CHAPTER 2

Teaching Oral Skills

My first experience as a second language learner occurred in 1961 when I was a high school freshman. That fall I entered John Kulas's first year French class and my life changed in ways I could never imagine at that time. Mr. Kulas was new to our school district, but not new to teaching. He was a product of several NDEA-funded summer language academies which emphasized audiolingual teaching, a very popular approach at that time, and one that still is widely used around the world. I remember him walking into our class that first day, introducing himself, then saying that for the next six weeks, we would not hear another word of English from him. Starting that day we drilled our way through sentence patterns, verb conjugations, and basic conversations. We sat through hours of listening to audiotapes of descriptions of French cultural institutions in a brand new language laboratory. I'm not so sure that my success in that class was due so much to the methodology as to the passion that Mr. Kulas brought with him for the French language and culture. Could I carry on a conversation in French as a result of this instruction? Probably at a minimal level. Could I read and write academic French prose? Probably better than I could speak it.

Eight years later, I entered my first Peace Corps training program on the campus of the University of Utah in Salt Lake City. There we were, 100 men, gathered there to learn how to be teachers of English as a foreign language in elementary schools throughout the desert Kingdom of Libya. Of course, not only were we there to learn how to teach English as a foreign lan-

guage, but we were also there to learn how to speak the Libyan dialect of Arabic. The methods used for both were rooted in the same principles of audiolingualism and structural linguistics that also grounded my French teacher, Mr. Kulas. Our materials had come from the University of Michigan, and it was several years later that I understood the connection of these materials to Charles Fries and Robert Lado, among others.

Sandwiched between those two experiences were opportunities I had for learning several more foreign languages, two to be exact. In the summer of 1964 I was selected to spend eight weeks as a participant of the American Field Service exchange program in southern Italy. During the ten-day voyage by ship from New York City to Rotterdam, those of us bound for Italy engaged in hours of cultural orientation and language learning. During the ensuing overnight train ride from Rotterdam to Naples, my mind was racing with thoughts of what to say, and how to behave. When I finally stepped off the train after nearly 48 hours, I was greeted by a wonderful family and was immediately swept up in the southern Italian community of Catanzaro from which I would emerge eight weeks later a changed person, but not much more conversant in Italian. The reason why was that my host father was quite fluent in English. He had studied English as a secondary student in Italy and honed his skills while a British prisoner of war in Egypt during the Second World War. It seems that many of the British soldiers were nearly illiterate and welcomed Filippo's skills when it came to writing letters home to England.

I continued my language learning experiences in college. Not only did I continue to study French, but I also studied Italian (to see just how much I may have learned subconsciously during that summer), and German.

Of all those languages, Arabic was by far the most difficult in which to gain any oral proficiency. Why was this so? After having been exposed to learning three languages, I felt confident that learning a fourth would not be difficult. It was only after some reflection of language teaching and learning that I began to assess effectiveness of methods and suitability for me as a *learner in different contexts. It is this personal foundation on which I started to build many of my assumptions about how adults in general learn a new language.*

Most adult ESL programs start by teaching adults how to speak English. The oral language becomes the foundation upon which literacy in the second language is constructed. So I begin my methods classes by focusing on the teaching of oral skills.

There are many schemes for categorizing language teaching methodology. And, in fact, there are many excellent resources that go into great detail in explaining one or the other typology. Richards and Rodgers (2001), Larsen-Freeman (2000), and Brown (2000) present several of the better known analyses of second language teaching methodology. Many of these texts discuss second language teaching from the perspective of the adult second language learner. But this perspective is heavily weighted in favor of the adult second language learner who has already achieved a relatively high level of formal education and is highly literate in the native language. Examples of these methodologies include grammar-translation, audiolingualism, and communicative language teaching. Others include the methods of the 1970s, including Community Language Learning (Curran, 1976; LaForge, 1971), Suggestopedia (Lozanov, 1979), The Silent Way (Gattegno, 1972), Total Physical Response (Asher, 1977), and the Natural Approach (Krashen, 1982).

These innovative methods have failed to catch on with the large majority of adult ESL teachers for a variety of reasons, with the possible exceptions of Total Physical Response (TPR) and the Natural Approach. Community Language Learning (CLL), with its philosophical roots in educational humanism, requires a highly trained facilitator, preferably one who is bilingual in the target language of instruction as well as the learner's home language. Since the content of instruction for the CLL class flows from the self-identified needs of the group members, there are no published materials appropriate for such a program. It assumes a homogeneous group of students with class size limited to 10 to 12 students in a group. The humanistic foundation of CLL is virtually identical to that of Knowles's principles of andragogy (Knowles & Associates, 1984). However, few adult ESL programs can offer the conditions of student homogeneity and small class size, along with the qualified bilingual facilitator. Regardless of its limitations, what we can take away from this language teaching approach is its emphasis on lowering learners' anxiety, building a mutually supportive learning community, and allowing learners the freedom to identify the language they want to learn.

The Silent Way has its roots in cognitive learning principles, and a strict philosophy of personal responsibility. Gattegno, the originator of The Silent Way, emphasizes problem solving and learner autonomy. What most observers of The Silent Way classroom remember is the use of manipulatives in the form of Cuisinaire rods, originally designed for teaching mathematical principles to children (not surprising as Gattegno himself was a mathematician). The other characteristic of The Silent Way classroom most often remembered by observers is the excruciating agony suffered by learners as they attempt to cope with the silence of the teacher. At the same time the major contributions of The Silent Way are the deemphasis on teacher talk and the focus on learner responsibility, concepts well worth considering with learners at any age.

According to Brown (2000), Suggestopedia, also called Desuggestopedia (Larsen-Freeman, 2000), developed from Soviet psychological research on the brain and its ability to function as a highly effective memory machine. A Suggestopedia classroom can be characterized by comfortable chairs and soft background music, preferably Baroque. Classroom techniques consist of role-play and games. Students are allowed to take on the identity of others, assuming the roles of native speakers. I observed a Suggestopedia classroom in Finland where students appeared to be enjoying the activities. When I asked the teacher why she thought this approach was so popular with her Finnish students, her response was, "The Finns are a shy people. This approach allows them the freedom to be someone else for a while." You won't find too many proponents of Suggestopedia in adult ESL programs in the United States. However, you will find examples of classrooms that incorporate games, music, and drama to provide a relaxing and enjoyable atmosphere for the adult learner.

One of my favorite authors, Earl Stevick, has written several extended accounts of his own experience with Community Language Learning, The Silent Way, and Suggestopedia, which he labels as "ways" (Stevick, 1980; 1998). According to Stevick (1998), each way is:

- radical. I mean this in the literal sense that each goes to the root of things to apply some single principle or set of related principles from the ground up.
- fresh. That is, each originated in thinking based outside the historical traditions, consensuses, and controversies of the language teaching profession.
- exceptionally effective, at least for some learners under at least some circumstances. (p. xiv)

I believe that what Stevick meant by this analysis is that these three methods represented radically new departures for language teachers. In fact, they have been referred to in the literature as revolutionary (Bodman, 1979) for how they brought to the field new insights into the process of second language learning that were diametrically opposed to the assumptions that supported other more dominant methods practiced at the time. What they have in common is that their originators were not so much interested in the language itself as interpreted by linguists, but were more interested in the processes of learning as studied by psychologists and as actually experienced by language learners. And for some learners, these radical departures from the traditional, or dominant, approaches to second language teaching were effective, although unfortunately little empirical evidence exists to support these claims. What can also be said is that there are vocal proponents of these methods, and very vocal opponents. What they all admit is that choosing a language teaching method is not a process of identifying a "one size fits all" method. Rather it is a thoughtful process of knowing the language learner and focusing on the individual needs of that learner.

Total Physical Response (TPR) is an approach with many more adherents among adult ESL teachers. It is usually classified as a comprehension approach. The casual observer might see links to behavioral principles of learning. Unlike audiolingualism, however, it does not require learners to produce language until they are ready to do so. Instead, TPR classrooms are characterized by the central role of the instructor and the focus on action verbs, or commands. "Stand up." "Sit down." "Turn around." "Point to your nose." These are commands that are both easily demonstrable and relevant to the vocabulary of the classroom. Comprehension is easily determined by observing the learners acting out the commands. Coupled with a language experience approach to literacy, it can be an effective approach to teaching basic oral language and building a foundation for early literacy skills in the adult ESL classroom. The creative teacher can teach very complex structures using this approach. However, in practice it is usually limited to the basic level classroom. Asher agreed with Curran that anxiety was a major stumbling block to adult learning. Both advocated allowing the learner to remain silent until ready to speak. And, like Gattegno and Lozanov, Asher believed in a multiple sensory approach, combining oral language with physical action.

Finally, the Natural Approach (Krashen & Terrell, 1983) is grounded in Krashen's (1982) theories of second language acquisition. The goal of the Natural Approach is the teaching of everyday language. The role of the teacher is to provide comprehensible input, or language that is slightly above the level of the learner's current language ability. Learners are not required to produce language until they are ready. The silent period in second language learning is similar to the silent period experienced in first language acquisition. TPR techniques are frequently used in initial stages of the Natural Approach. The classroom is characterized by an abundance of pictures, real-life objects (realia), and printed language, similar to what you might find in an elementary classroom, but suitable for adult learners.

In summary, these five approaches to second language teaching offer unique insights into the teaching of adult English language learners. The skillful teacher should at least be aware of these approaches and choose the most appropriate strategies. They represent widely contrasting views of learning and educational philosophies. But in the diversity of the adult ESL classroom, we must have a large toolbox to meet the needs of all of our students.

Speaking of large toolboxes, TESOL (2003) has recently published its *Standards for Adult Education ESL Programs.* Standard 3 focuses on instruction. According to this standard, effective instruction of adult ESL rests on the following principles:

- Adult learners bring a variety of experiences, skills, and knowledge to the classroom that need to be acknowledged and included in lessons.
- Language acquisition is facilitated through providing a nonthreatening environment in which learners feel comfortable and self-confident and are encouraged to take risks to use the target language.
- Adult learners progress more rapidly when the content is relevant to their lives.
- Language learning is cyclical, not linear, so learning objectives need to be recycled in a variety of contexts. (p. 20)

These principles form the foundation of the instructional approaches proposed next in the *Standards.* These approaches include the following:

- Grammar-based (focus on language structure)
- Competency-based or functional (focus on specific tasks needed in everyday life)
- Whole language (focus on all communication skills, with particular emphasis on written language)
- Participatory (focus on personal empowerment and social change)
- Content-based (focus on language in specific content areas, such as vocational training or citizenship)
- Project-based (focus on group or collaborative learning) (pp. 20–21)

Given the learning principles and instructional approaches, the *Standards* go on to characterize effective language teaching. These characteristics include the following:

- Active learning
- Focus on language used in the classroom and beyond
- Integration of all communication skills
- Accommodation of different learning styles
- Grouping strategies and interaction
- Attention to the needs of the multilevel classroom
- Focus on learning strategies, such as problem solving, team building, and critical thinking
- Use of authentic language
- Integration of appropriate technologies
- Integration of language and culture
- Preparation of students for a variety of authentic assessment activities (p. 21)

THE EVOLUTION OF AN ADULT ESL EDUCATOR

I can describe my own development as a second language educator of adults as occurring in three stages. What follows is a discussion of those three stages and how each stage reflects the broad characteristics of language teaching as described above. The first stage reflects my introduction to the field and my initial training in the principles of audiolingualism in the late 1960s. The second stage reflects my early years as a teacher educator in the late 1970s into the 1980s and my adherence to the principles of communicative language teaching. The third stage, beginning in the mid 1980s, shows my interest in more participatory approaches and my concern for social justice issues of the language learner and the language teacher. After discussing the three stages of my development along with sample scenarios of teaching practice, I will provide an analysis of the three stages as manifested in the scenarios, using the characteristics of effective instruction as listed under Standard 3 of the TESOL Standards (TESOL, 2003).

Stage One

I was introduced to second language teaching both as a learner and as a teacher in the years when audiolingualism dominated the field. Throughout the 1960s, educational psychology was highly influenced by behaviorism. Behaviorism was found in second language teaching in the form of pattern practice, repetitive drilling, and inductive learning. Practice sentence patterns long enough and you too will achieve perfection. Trouble was, comprehension took a back seat to perfect pronunciation and intonation and was to come only later in the process of language learning.

Audiolingualism grew out of a political and social context which found the United States alone at the top of the world following World War II, the major industrialized nation to escape annihilation of its infrastructure. We were the only nation with the resources to give leadership, both militarily and economically, to the rebuilding of both East and West. The trouble was, we had for so long practiced an isolationist foreign policy that we were not prepared with personnel who spoke the languages of the many countries where we now found ourselves.

At this same time, a small group of American linguists had already started to combine the elements of structural linguistics and behavioral psychology to give the field a new language teaching methodology referred to originally as the Army Method, later the audiolingual method (ALM), and also by some as the Michigan Method. The field of second language acquisition research was only in its infancy. What these linguists did was think intuitively about how children learn their first language, and try to apply what they thought to be true about first language acquisition to the development of this radically new second language teaching methodology. ALM became the first attempt to apply "scientific-based research" to second language teaching (Fries, 1945). To this day, elements of audiolingualism dominate second language teaching around the globe, even though the method and the principles upon which it is based have lost a great deal of favor in North America.

At the University of Michigan, Charles Fries and Robert

Lado applied this new methodology to the development of a curriculum for a new Intensive English Institute. Here they found some success with ALM. Keep in mind, though, that the students who came to their Intensive English Institute were well prepared for the rigors of this methodology. They were highly educated in their first language, highly motivated to learn English so as to access the institutions of higher education in the United States, and for the most part disciplined to handle the highly repetitive nature of the many drills and exercises that became the core of ALM.

Peace Corps relied on ALM to teach its many volunteers through the 1960s. Since many of the early Peace Corps programs were designed to train educators of English as a foreign language, not only were the volunteers themselves taught the home languages of the countries where they were assigned, but many of us were taught to use ALM in teaching English to the tens of thousands of our students through the decade. It is for this reason, I believe, that ALM grew to have such a widespread appeal and use, so that, even now, it influences not only the teaching methods but also the materials designed for use in the second language classroom around the world.

ALM offered a distinct advantage compared to other more traditional foreign language teaching methodologies of the day (primarily grammar-translation). This advantage was that it did not require a highly trained linguist or educator to be relatively successful with this method. In the 1960s Peace Corps programs recruited primarily freshly graduated college students with bachelor's degrees to be volunteers. In fact, the less we knew of the language of the assigned country the better, because they were going to teach us how to speak that language. And the less we knew about teaching methodology the better, because they were going to train us to use their methodology.

Let me now take you into a classroom where the teacher is using ALM. This is an institute in Tunis, Tunisia, affiliated with the University of Tunis, but with the primary mission to provide primarily noncredit continuing education in a variety of foreign languages to any adults willing and able to pay for the opportunity. The class I will describe is a beginning level English classroom taught in the evening. The students are all adults over the age of 18. Some of the younger students are university students. Many of the older adults are working professionals, such as bankers, police officers, and other government functionaries. Some of the women are housewives, either European or Tunisian, and don't work outside the home. For them, this class is an important social outlet. The older adults come from several different first language backgrounds, but primarily French and Arabic. Instruction in this class is entirely in English, the target language (L2).

Teacher: *Listen! Don't speak!* (The teacher signals to the students, as in a game of Charades, by putting a finger first to the ear, then to the mouth. The students all appear to understand what they are to do.)

Teacher: *Brian and Ali are walking down the street. They see their friend Ahmad with someone they have not met. They greet, then Ahmad introduces his friend to Brian and Ali.*

Ahmad: *Brian and Ali, this is Georges. Georges, this is Brian and Ali.*

Georges: *Pleased to meet you.*

Brian: *It's our pleasure. Where are you from?*

Georges: *I'm from Paris, but I work in Tunis.*

Ali: *We hope you are enjoying your stay in Tunis.*

Georges: *Yes, very much.*

Ahmad: *We have to go now. We're late for class. See you later!*

Brian and Ali: *Yes, see you!*

The teacher repeats this dialogue several times, each time displaying a picture of the four students so that they know who is speaking when. The teacher asks for volunteers and eventually all of the students take a part. The teacher then moves into a series of drills, using patterns taken from the dialogue, but gradually introducing new vocabulary. The teacher leads the drills, signaling to the students to repeat. Gradually the teacher moves to a new drill, called a substitution drill, in which the students respond by substituting new words in the structure according to a designed cue. The teacher uses a combination of hand signals and pictures to indicate to the students how they are to respond. They do not see the written dialogue.

Teacher: *Brian and Ali, this is Georges. Repeat!*
Students: *Brian and Ali, this is Georges.* (They repeat this structure several times following the teacher's model).
Teacher: *Brian and Ali, this is Mary. Repeat!* (The teacher holds up a picture of a young woman.)
Students: *Brian and Ali, this is Mary.*
Teacher: *Brian and Ali, this is Ahmad.* (Teacher holds a picture of a young man.)
Students: *Brian and Ali, this is Ahmad.*
After many repetitions until the teacher is satisfied that the students can control this structure, the class moves to the substitution exercise.
Teacher: *Brian and Ali, this is Georges.* Cue: *Mary*
Teacher: *Brian and Ali, this is Mary.* (The teacher uses a picture of Mary to convey meaning to the students.)
Teacher: *Brian and Ali, this is Georges.* Cue: *Mary*
Students: *Brian and Ali, this is Mary.*
Teacher: *Ahmad.* (The teacher holds a picture of Ahmad.)
Students: *Brian and Ali, this is Ahmad.*
Teacher: *Mahmoud.* (The teacher holds a picture of Mahmoud.)
Students: *Brian and Ali, this is Mahmoud.*
The teacher moves to a new structure from the dialogue.
Teacher: *Where are you from? Repeat!*
Students: *Where are you from?*
After multiple repetitions, the teacher signals a new drill. This time, instead of substituting words, they are going to answer the question.
Teacher: *Where are you from?* Cue: *Paris*
Students: *I'm from Paris.*
Teacher: *Where are you from?* Cue: *Tunis*
Students: *I'm from Tunis.*
Teacher: *Where are you from?* Cue: *London*
Students: *I'm from London.*
Following many repetitions, the teacher drills individual students.
Teacher to Student 1: *Where are you from?* Cue (while holding a picture of Tunis): *Tunis*
Student 1: (quickly catching on to the change in the pattern) *I'm from Tunis.*

Teacher to Student 2: *Where are you from?* Cue (with picture of a familiar landmark): *London*
Student 2: *I'm from London.*
Teacher to Student 3: *Where are you from?* Cue (with picture): *Paris*
Student 3: *I'm from Paris.*
After many repetitions, the teacher moves to a new structure. After about 10 minutes of drilling, the teacher comes back to the original dialogue. By this time the students have it memorized and can stand in groups of four to act it out in front of the others.

Stage Two

By the time I started work as a teacher educator in the late 1970s, the field of second language teaching was working under a new set of assumptions about language teaching and language learning. In the decade of the 70s, the assumptions of behaviorism had lost favor among language educators and were replaced by the assumptions of cognitivism and humanism. But more importantly, the demographics of the adult second language learning population in the United States and Canada had begun to change dramatically. With the end of the Vietnam conflict in 1975, the United States and Canada began to receive tens of thousands of refugees from Vietnam, Laos, and Cambodia. And what was even more significant about these refugees was their educational histories. Many of them had limited formal schooling in their first languages. Many from Laos, the Hmong, were not even literate in their first language. The language teaching community in the United States and Canada was not prepared for these new learners. Meanwhile, political events in Central and South America were beginning to push a stream of refugees north across the southern borders of the United States. These refugees were fleeing economic hardship and political persecution and looking for a better life in "El Norte."

Another change was related to developments in the European community of second language teachers. Europe, primarily

England, France, and Germany, had started to attract a growing number of immigrants, "guest workers," from North Africa, Turkey, and elsewhere around the Mediterranean. These immigrants were seeking jobs in the more robust economies of Europe. The Council of Europe was leading the charge in developing new curricula to assist these migrant workers to succeed in the factories of Europe. The language teaching community was beginning to focus attention on communicative language teaching (Brumfit & Johnson, 1979; Widdowson, 1978). Linguists were turning their attention to the notions of competence and performance (Hymes, 1971). Whereas earlier ALM classrooms focused on performance, teaching the rules of the language, the communicative classroom would focus on competence, knowing how to actually use the language in a variety of contexts.

The following scenario could have taken place in an intermediate to advanced level classroom with adult ESL learners in the United States in the late 1970s. Imagine this class being held in a community college. The teacher is working part-time, is a college-educated female, and has had only minimal training in teaching ESL. The students are a combination of Mexican and Vietnamese, all of whom have been living in the United States for more than two years. They work in entry-level jobs in local factories, jobs that do not require much literacy. However, these students want to improve their speaking abilities in order to carry on conversations with native English speakers. They want to be more effective consumers in the local stores, especially the grocery stores where the foods are so strange and new to them. They also have children in the local schools and are very uncomfortable with the notion that their children are learning English faster than they are. This is putting the parents into the very awkward position of depending on the children for news about what is happening in their schools and in the community. Although the emphasis in this class is on speaking and listening, the observer will note that printed English is included in the lesson. In fact, it is more difficult here to separate the instruction of only one or two communication skills. This method assumes an integration of all the communication skills from the very beginning.

In this class, the teacher has been basing the lessons on authentic materials she has found in the community that the students have expressed an interest in. In this particular lesson, she is teaching some consumer economics. The vocabulary comes from the foods found in the grocery store. She has also brought into the classroom newspaper advertising giving information about sales in the grocery store that week.

The teacher greets all of the students as they enter the classroom. With each one she asks them how they are, and how their children are. The students have all worked a long day in their jobs and are tired, but they still show enthusiasm for the class.

The teacher begins the lesson by giving some general directions to the students. She tells them that tonight's lesson would focus on shopping at the local grocery store. She has put on the table in front of all of the students a number of food products and packages from the grocery store. Some are fresh fruits and vegetables. Some are canned products. She asks the students for the names of the fresh fruits and vegetables. She is able to get a response from most of them. She writes the names on the chalkboard and has a picture of the item that she can tape to the chalkboard next to the name.

Next, she holds up an advertisement from the local newspaper that gives sales information for that week. She asks her students if any of them read this advertisement before they go shopping. No one raises a hand.

She then divides the class into small groups for the first activity. There are 20 students in class that night. She divides them into five small groups of four each. She makes sure that each group has speakers of both Spanish and Vietnamese, to the extent possible. Their first assignment is to create a short dialogue, something they think they might need to say to an English speaker in the grocery store if they are having difficulty finding a particular item.

During this time, the teacher walks around the room, listening to each group, answering questions, and offering suggestions. After about 30 minutes, the teacher brings this activity to a halt and asks each group to act out their dialogues. As each group acts out their dialogues, the teacher writes the dialogues on the chalkboard. Once all of the dialogues have been presented, she then goes over each one providing a little feedback on a particular structure or vocabulary item. The end result is a dialogue that is more authentic, as if spoken by native speakers.

The final activity is a game based on the advertisement from the newspaper. She divides the class into pairs. To one member of each pair, she gives a question. To the other member of each pair she gives answers. But the answers must be found in the advertisement. Only one choice is appropriate for each question. After they finish this phase of the activity, they reverse roles. The student who had been given the questions is now given the answers. The other student is given a new set of questions.

After finishing these exercises, the teacher reviews with the students the original dialogues that the students produced at the beginning of the lesson. Back in their original groups of four, the students now must develop a role play in which one student represents the shopkeeper, and the other three students represent customers. Their instruction from the teacher is to develop a dialogue which includes several names of the foods they were introduced to earlier in the evening, together with at least two pieces of information that were part of the second exercise. The students perform these role plays which ends the class for that evening.

Stage Three

The 1970s were a decade of more than revolutionary changes in language teaching methodology. It was also a decade of revolutionary changes in general educational philosophy. One figure who crossed boundaries between adult educators and second language teaching in North America was Paulo Freire (1970). By the mid-1980s, Freire's influence was growing among a small group of adult educators in ESL programs who were concerned that the living and working conditions of the new immigrants was making it impossible for them to learn. In some cases, they worked in unsafe conditions and lived in substandard housing. For the new immigrants, many either didn't know the difference or were simply afraid to confront their employers for fear of losing their jobs, or their landlords for fear of losing their housing. Immigration continued to grow by leaps and bounds into the 1990s, and while the general economy was growing, these immigrants were cautiously welcomed. It was also clear during this time that many of these new immigrants were undocumented. This was particularly true for many of those coming into the United States from Mexico and other countries in Central and South America.

At the same time, an increasing number of adult ESL teachers were growing impatient with their own working conditions. Program providers across the nation had grown to rely largely on part-time educators. Many of these part-timers had acquired advanced degrees and considerable experience, but were limited to part-time jobs with no benefits. The growing concern among adult ESL educators for both their own professional environments and the work and living environments of their students caused many to support an approach to education known variously as participatory or critical pedagogy.

Programs that supported a participatory approach to adult ESL are usually found in urban areas, and are supported by community-based agencies. The teachers aren't always trained teachers, but perhaps ideally they come from the same communities as their learners. In fact, the teachers are themselves products of these same programs, or similar programs. In addition to teaching language and communication skills, these programs also teach the students their legal rights within the community and at the workplace. Participatory approaches to adult ESL came originally from the work of Freire in his native Brazil, and later in other South American countries, Africa, and elsewhere. Programs most likely to be attracted to the participatory philosophy of Freire are those that work with the least educated and the most vulnerable within our society. I began to look more closely at this approach in the mid 1980s at the same time that I was researching part-time issues of adult educators working in ESL. A few materials were being published at the time which took a critical look at the living and working conditions of immigrants, especially in urban settings. One of the first published attempts to provide an analysis of this approach was Waller-stein's *Language and Culture in Conflict* (1983).

The following lesson scenario could take place anywhere, but imagine it taking place in a community-based program in a large urban center. There are 15 adult learners, all from Mexico and several other Central American countries. All are undocumented and have been living in the United States for one to five years. They work entry-level jobs, several as housekeepers in one of the larger hotels in the city, or in a local plastics factory where they do piece work at minimum wage. With few exceptions they have attended schools in their native countries, but only for three or four years of elementary school. Most have children who attend the public schools in their community. The instructor has a college education but is not a trained educator. Born in Mexico, she grew up in the same urban community, is a naturalized U.S. citizen, and works part-time as a Spanish-language bilingual translator for the county judicial system.

The curriculum for this program is based on a participatory philosophy (Auerbach, 1992; 1996) in which students generate the topics, and the major goal of the program is to empower the students not only in their relationships with employers, but also in their relationships with their children's schools. Recently one of the students, Maria, started a new job as a home school liaison for her children's bilingual program. She really enjoys this work. Her supervising teacher has also expressed an interest in helping her to attend a local community college where she could be trained and certified as a bilingual teacher assistant, thus helping her to increase her income and gain some stability in her work. The problem is that Maria is not documented, she used a false Social Security number to gain her present employment, and she anticipates that her status will be discovered soon. What are her rights, if any, and what can she do to change her status?

The teacher decides to use this problem as a basis for a lesson on immigrant rights, the Immigration and Naturalization Service, and other related issues that cause great concern among her students every day. In this first lesson, the class will focus on discussing, in their native Spanish and using whatever

English they know, what questions they have, what they already know, and what they want to know about their status and the rights of their children to attend school. They have heard that a state legislator has talked about possibly requiring schools to identify children who are undocumented. These parents know that if this happens, they will be forced to keep their children at home, or they will be forced to move to another state. They have all decided that they cannot return to their native countries and home communities where jobs are not available and where their children would not have any opportunity to get an education.

Based on the questions that surface in this first session, the teacher decides to use the contacts she has developed through her work in the courts. She plans to bring in several experts from an advocacy organization called the Coalition of Immigrant and Refugee Rights to talk to the students. In preparation for these visits, the teacher works with the students to develop questions and practice how to ask these questions in English. Later, as a result of these sessions, the students decide that they should start to write letters to others in positions of power who might be sympathetic to their plight. The letters need to be written in English, as they will be sent to a number of people who do not speak or read Spanish. Never does the teacher talk about grammar. Rather, she structures her lessons to facilitate discussion and action that will help the students to find answers to their questions with the hope of solving some of these problems. The immediate problem is helping Maria start the teacher certification program in the local community college, because the students know she would make an excellent bilingual teacher for their children.

ANALYSIS

Table 2.1 provides an analysis of how each of these scenarios presented above reflect to a greater or lesser degree the characteristics of effective instruction that are listed under Standard 3 of the TESOL Standards for Adult ESL Programs (TESOL, 2003).

Table 2.1 Analysis of Scenarios across Three Stages using Characteristics of Effective Instruction from Standard Three of the TESOL Standards for Adult ESL Programs (TESOL, 2003).

Characteristics of Effective Instruction	Stage One	Stage Two	Stage Three
1. Learners take an active role in the learning process.	On surface, students appear to be actively engaged. However, many responses rely on rote memorization. Teacher controls direction of drill.	Students are engaged in various activities. The teacher recognizes the knowledge they already have by asking them to generate initial dialogues.	Entire curriculum evolves from needs of the learners. This helps to ensure an active role on their part in the learning process.
2. Learners acquire communication skills necessary for functioning in and out of the classroom.	Dialogues that begin lesson contain sentence patterns and vocabulary that students may find useful outside the classroom.	Dialogues represent authentic language structures and vocabulary that students have heard and already know.	Focus of class activities is totally on enabling learners to acquire and use communication skills with problems they have identified.
3. Activities integrate the four language skills.	Only oral language is promoted in early stages. No written language is used to reinforce oral language.	Listening and speaking are quickly integrated with reading and writing in this lesson.	Activities integrate the language skills appropriate to learners' needs. In this lesson, all four language skills are integrated from the start.
4. Activities address different learning styles and special needs of learners.	Final repetition of dialogue in small groups engages students. But there appears to be no effort to address different learning styles, or the special needs of certain students.	Instructor addresses different learning styles by use of authentic, tangible materials. Use of cooperative learning is encouraged.	Instructor uses learners' native language to set the stage, to identify the problem to be posed, and to ensure comprehension of major issues.

Table 2.1 *Continued*

Characteristics of Effective Instruction	Stage One	Stage Two	Stage Three
5. Activities incorporate grouping strategies and interactive tasks.	There may be grouping, but drills are based on highly structured dialogues. Students do not necessarily develop their own dialogues.	Groups develop dialogues that turn into role-plays. Pair activities include information gap exercises.	The lesson starts with problem posing. Lessons include cooperative learning and role plays, which help learners practice how to use language in different situations.
6. Activities take into account the needs of different levels of learners.	All students are highly educated in a first language to begin with. Little attention is given to differentiated instruction.	Teacher shows interest in all students from moment they enter class. Students are grouped to mix languages and ability levels.	Teacher accounts for needs of multi-level learners through use of the native language as a tool for facilitating comprehension of issues.
7. Activities focus on development of language and culturally appropriate behaviors.	Dialogues help to contextualize the language. However, there is little overt effort to teach critical thinking and problem solving skills.	This lesson focuses not only on culturally appropriate behaviors, but also on language needed for critical thinking and problem solving.	Language focuses on developing culturally appropriate behaviors to empower learners. The language that is needed to enable learners is viewed as a means to an end, rather than an end in itself.
8. Activities allow learners to use authentic resources both inside and outside classroom.	The only authentic language is found in the dialogue. Since focus of instruction is on oral language only, there is no effort at this point to bring in examples of authentic written materials.	Authentic materials are integral to this lesson.	Teacher uses authentic outside resources, such as guest speakers, who can share their knowledge with the learners. Students are considered important resources themselves.

Table 2.1 *Continued*

Characteristics of Effective Instruction	Stage One	Stage Two	Stage Three
9. Activities enable learners to develop awareness and competency in use of appropriate technologies.	There is no effort to develop awareness in technologies other than those used in the process of instruction.	Use of technologies is not a requirement for successful implementation of this lesson. But they could be incorporated with little effort, if available.	This lesson does not overtly give learners opportunities to develop skills in the use of technologies, but that could be more due to limited resources than to basic assumptions of instruction.
10. Activities are culturally sensitive.	One could argue that the dialogue is an effort to integrate language and culture. But since the teacher focuses only on the structures and vocabulary, it is up to the students to infer cultural context.	These activities appear to be culturally sensitive. Students are not only introduced to authentic situations; they are also encouraged to build dialogues using vocabulary that is part of their everyday life.	The language and aspects of culture integrated into these lessons are chosen by the learners themselves and supported by the expertise of the facilitator who comes from the community of the learners.
11. Activities prepare learners for formal and informal assessment situations.	Students are assessed in terms of how they can use the language in authentic conversation, but in tightly controlled sentence structures. The highly controlled vocabulary and structures taught in these lessons lend themselves to use of formal, standardized assessment processes.	Teacher is engaged in informal assessment while walking among the students. Information gap activities provide more such opportunities. Curricula based on communicative teaching incorporate opportunities for formal assessment as well.	Students are engaged in self-assessment. Formal assessment would not be appropriate in this approach. Success is measured by how well students achieve personal and group goals they themselves identify at the beginning of the lesson.

SUMMARY

My own development as an adult educator has paralleled to some degree the development of many methods of teaching oral skills to adults over the decades since 1969. Awareness of these many methodologies has encouraged me to reflect on my own teaching and my basic assumptions about second language learning and teaching. I have evolved in my own thinking from a focus on language (the content of instruction), to a focus on communication (language use), to a focus on the students and the multiple roles they bring to the teaching/learning transaction.

This chapter provides an introduction to several broad categories of adult ESL instructional approaches. Three different classroom scenarios are offered, followed by an analysis of each using criteria that can be found in the TESOL standards for adult ESL programs recently published by TESOL, Inc. Each scenario reflects a distinctly different approach to teaching adult English language learners that I have experienced over the course of my own career in the field. We need to consider the basic assumptions underlying each of these approaches and build on knowledge gained from understanding how adults acquire additional languages to develop their own effective instructional approaches.

In the next chapter, we will look at approaches to teaching reading and writing to adult English language learners. But first we will examine what we mean by literacy in the 21st century.

CHAPTER 3

Teaching Literacy Skills

Literacy is using printed and written information to function in society, to achieve one's goals, and to develop one's knowledge and potential.

2003 National Assessment of
Adult Literacy

Literacy is not first and foremost a mental possession of individuals. Rather, it is first and foremost a social relationship among people, their ways with words, deeds, and things, and their institutions. Literacy is primarily and fundamentally out in the social, historical, cultural, and political world. It is only secondarily a set of cognitive skills, skills which subserve literacies as social acts in quite diverse ways in different contexts.

J. P. Gee, in Kalmar (2001, p. iv)

Although the ability to speak English is often the primary focus of adult ESL classrooms, the ability to read and write in the context of performing adult roles is fast becoming the standard by which success in adult ESL programs is measured. Given the importance of literacy in evaluating success of instruction in adult ESL, it is no wonder that the definition of what we call literacy becomes so important, and that literacy itself has become a lightening rod for political debate.

Literacy is now widely used to describe multiple competencies (such as computer literacy or cultural literacy) and is the standard by which federally funded programs are assessed. Literacy became a topic of concern of the general public in the 1980s, prompted largely by reports from the National Commission on Excellence in Education (1983) and the National Education Goals Panel (1993) challenging the nation to become fully literate by the year 2000. Within the current context of national education legislation, reading has been given new emphasis as the basic building block for all learning (National Reading Panel, 2000).

This emphasis on literacy in the schools and society, beginning with the emergent literacy taught to small children in their first language, to the different literacies taught in adult education, should cause us to pause and examine what we mean by literacy. Is literacy the ability to decode letters and words? Does literacy include the ability to write as well as read? What does it mean to equate literacy and competency, as in computer literacy? Is learning to be literate a political act? Does acquiring literacy assume the acquisition of self-empowerment? If so, what does that mean? Is it fair to say that beginning English language learners are illiterate even though they may be literate in their first language? Understanding what we mean by literacy will help us to better understand how to teach others to be literate.

Anyone who has been following the developments in education recently can't help but notice the emphasis placed on empirical evidence from scientifically based research for supporting choices in literacy instruction and materials. Most of the research, however, has been done with children learning to read in a first language (National Reading Panel, 2000; Snow, Burns, & Griffin, 1998), with adult first-language literacy learners (Kruidenier, 2002), or with adult English language learners enrolled in college or intensive English programs (Burt, Peyton, & Adams, 2003). Few studies (Kalmar, 2001) have examined the unique needs of adult English language learners who may be illiterate or semiliterate in their first language.

If we examine the history of adult education in the United States, we can see that the teaching of literacy has been a major focus of informal adult education. Usually the teaching of literacy has been coupled with other life skills, such as job skills, or religious training, or citizenship. The federal government's involvement in adult education starting in 1966 has centered on literacy education and workforce preparation. The 1998 re-authorization of the law funding adult education was called the Adult Education and Family Literacy Act, Title II of the Work-force Investment Act (P.L. 105-220). Given the language of the next version of this law (U.S. Department of Education, 2003), it is important that adult educators increase their awareness of the research base that supports their instruction (Burt, Peyton, & Adams, 2003).

It is fair to say that literacy instruction of adult English language learners has been shaped by many of the approaches used to teach oral skills, such as audiolingual and communica-tive language teaching. These approaches reflect changes in how we understand the nature of language learning in general. It wasn't until the 1970s, however, that other developments in edu-cation began to emerge that would help to shape literacy educa-tion as we know it today. The fact that many of these under-standings of literacy were so diametrically opposed to each other only reinforced the debate that has raged in the field of literacy. In the 1970s three individuals and their publications influenced my own conceptions of teaching literacy skills in adult basic education. Each continues to have profound effects on how adult educators approach their own teaching of literacy to adults.

COMPETENCY-BASED LITERACY EDUCATION

The first of these three individuals is Norvel Northcutt. Be-ginning in 1971, he led a team of researchers in a study funded by the U.S. Office of Education called the Adult Performance Level (APL) Project. It introduced the concept of competency-based education to the field of adult basic education (Sticht & Armstrong, 1994). The APL Project identified five areas of knowledge considered important for an adult to function suc-cessfully in mainstream American society. These areas included occupational knowledge, consumer economics, health, commu-

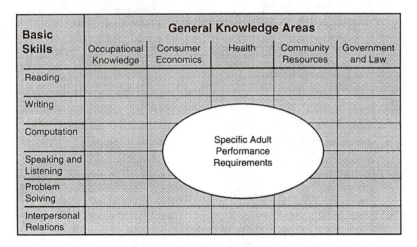

Basic Skills	General Knowledge Areas				
	Occupational Knowledge	Consumer Economics	Health	Community Resources	Government and Law
Reading					
Writing					
Computation		Specific Adult Performance Requirements			
Speaking and Listening					
Problem Solving					
Interpersonal Relations					

Figure 3.1 The Adult Performance Level Curriculum Matrix

nity resources, and government and law. In addition to these knowledge areas, the APL Project identified skills considered to be important for successful functioning. These skill areas included reading, writing, computation, speaking and listening, problem solving, and interpersonal relations. The scope of this report was such that the U.S. Department of Education was seriously considering revamping the entire GED curriculum to adopt a competency-based model similar to what the APL Project proposed.

Figure 3.1 provides a curriculum matrix that could be used with the basic knowledge areas and skills identified by the Adult Performance Level Project. Fill in each blank square with a competency that would reflect the knowledge and skill for that interaction. You can modify your own curriculum according to your local needs.

Since 1977, competency-based approaches to adult literacy instruction have been widely incorporated into classroom materials and staff development. A competency is usually defined as a task that the learner is to be able to perform. Evaluation of successful learning is based on observation of the task being performed satisfactorily. Based on notions of learning as a function of doing, and assessment based on observation of the performance, competency-based education has its roots in behaviorism. Proponents often claim that competency-based education is learner-centered, because the tasks are those representing real-life skills required of the learner to be successful in their everyday lives (Savage, 1993). Although in theory, selection of tasks is to be made only after a careful needs assessment of the learner, critics of competency-based education like to point out that selection of tasks is more often not made by the learner, but by the curriculum developer, or materials writer, or funding agency.

The APL Project initially targeted only adult basic education programs. Then, soon after its inception, the United States began receiving thousands of Southeast Asian refugees. The popularity of competency-based education soon led to its application to the development of curriculum for teaching these new English language learners. In fact, by the time the initial APL Project was completed in 1977, two-thirds of the states had adopted competency-based approaches in programs of adult literacy instruction.

Competency-based education supports many of the more recent approaches to teaching English language learners. These approaches include instruction in task-based, work-based, and general survival skills. Instructional objectives are described as tasks or competencies. Some of these competencies might include following directions, filling out forms, reading food labels, understanding classified ads, making appointments, and writing a check. The competency statement commonly begins with the stem "students will be able to . . . " Verbs are carefully selected that convey the sense of a measurable action. For instance, verbs such as *understand* or *appreciate* do not lend themselves readily to measurable objectives. Evaluation of learning is based on how well the student can demonstrate mastery of the stated competency.

The most recent iteration of a competency-based curriculum with implications for adult ESL would be Equipped for the Future (EFF), an initiative of the National Institute for Literacy (NIFL) (Stein, 2000). A close look at this report reveals that its roots can be traced back to the APL Project of 1977. Equipped for the Future emerged as a response to the National Education Goals Panel challenge for a literate nation by 2000 (National Education Goals Panel, 1993). NIFL surveyed teachers and adult learners across the country to ask them how they would respond to Goal 6: What is it that adults need to know and be able to do in order to be literate, compete in the global economy, exercise the rights and responsibilities of citizenship and participate fully in their children's education? From these responses emerged the four purposes for learning:

1. Access to information and resources so adults can orient themselves in the world (communication skills).

2. Action to be able to solve problems and make decisions, acting independently (decision-making skills).

3. Voice to express ideas and opinions with the confidence that one will be heard and taken into account. (interpersonal skills).

4. Bridge to the future to learn how to learn in order to keep up with the world as it changes (lifelong learning skills) (Stein, 1995).

These four purposes are further subdivided into 16 content standards (see Figure 3.2). EFF encourages teachers and learners to consider how to learn these skills and thereby enable learners to achieve their educational goals. Furthermore, programs need to help learners to identify barriers to learning and develop strategies for getting around them. This framework developed by EFF provides a link between curriculum and instruction and assessment and evaluation that can help the adult learner achieve real-world outcomes (Marshall, 2002), and will likely influence adult ESL curriculum development in the near future.

PARTICIPATORY ADULT LITERACY

The second individual to have a profound effect on my understanding of adult literacy is Paulo Freire. The publication

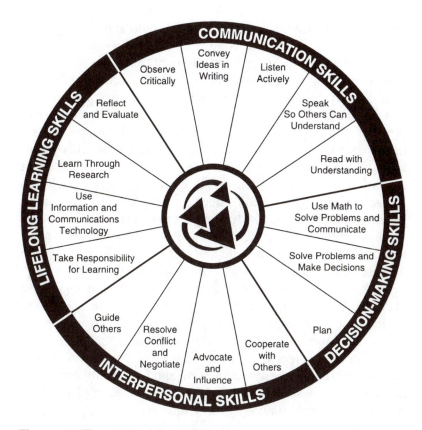

Figure 3.2 The 16 Equipped for the Future content standards (Stein, 2000, p. 21)

that continues to be cited for framing the basic constructs of Freire's notion of adult literacy is *Pedagogy of the Oppressed* (1970). For Freire, acquiring literacy skills is a political act. The ability of adults to name their world through the printed word is an emancipatory act that is usually required before adults can gain control over oppressive political, economic, and social forces. This category of adult literacy program is commonly labeled *participatory*, because it implies a genuine participation of the learner in all phases of learning. Furthermore, it requires an equality of status between learner and teacher, such that both are often referred to as co-learners. Participatory literacy education is the antithesis of most other common approaches to literacy instruction, including competency-based literacy education.

From a Freirian perspective, literacy education that is limited to workforce development or survival skills acquisition would likely be interpreted as a form of domestication. For Freirian adult educators, learning literacy is much more than simple skills acquisition. It is a process of self-empowerment. In their view, limiting the definition of literacy to skills acquisition explains the high attrition rates in conventional adult education programs. In contrast to conventional approaches to literacy, participatory adult educators would argue that adult learners must be engaged in a struggle to identify what is meaningful in their lives (Spener, 1993; 1994). They need to understand the nature of economic and political forces that seek to perpetuate the current power relationships that divide the haves and the have nots. Whether or not you agree with the ideological perspective of this approach, it is difficult to argue against the notion that the learner lies at the center of instruction.

Freire's continuing influence on the field can be seen in largely urban centers with the emergence of participatory programs working primarily with Latino and Caribbean immigrant populations. These programs tend to be community-based and rely relatively little on government subsidy.

WHOLE LANGUAGE

The third person to affect my own thinking about teaching literacy, and who had a profound effect on the teaching of reading in general, is Frank Smith. His book *Understanding Reading: A Psycholinguistic Analysis of Reading and Learning to Read* (1971), now in its sixth edition, introduced me to the emerging discipline of psycholinguistics. Smith and others attempted to provide the field of reading with a scientifically based set of principles that ran counter to the prevailing notions of skills-based instruction, most commonly phonics. The teaching approach that would come to be identified with the findings of this discipline is commonly labeled *whole language*.

Whole language has also been a focal point for many critics of reading instruction. Its top-down approach, starting with whole texts that are meaningful for the learner, is often blamed for low reading achievement. Opponents of whole language can be found among politicians and their many constituent groups. Brinkley (1998) argues for a connection of reading pedagogy and religious fundamentalism when she writes:

> Parents of the religious right, comparing what they hear with their own school memories, are also likely to be influenced by a deluge of anti-whole language mail they receive regularly from at least half a dozen nationally organized religious-right groups, such as Citizens for Excellence in Education, Concerned Women of America, and the Eagle Forum. (p. 57)

Whole language advocates believe that you introduce the learner to literature that will hold their interest, whether that be a comic book, the sports page, or Harry Potter.

According to Brinkley, whole language critics focus on three elements or flashpoints (p. 58): phonics versus whole language; invented spelling; and basal readers versus literature. Brinkley, and other whole language advocates, contend that English language learners are often disadvantaged by an early reliance on phonics for reading instruction, primarily because of the irregular spellings and variable correspondence between letters and sounds found in so many basic English language sight words. Instead, teachers of English language learners have found it necessary to focus on language in context, whether that context be the classroom or the workplace. Goodman (1986) summarized the arguments of the whole language proponents using the comparisons found in Figure 3.3.

The language experience approach (Stauffer, 1965) has demonstrated success with many adult English language learners with limited first language literacy and limited formal schooling (Dixon & Nessel, 1983; Rigg & Kazemek, 1993). Although its introduction to the literature of reading instruction preceded Smith's earliest work, language experience reflects the same assumptions of whole language as outlined by Goodman in Figure 3.3.

IT'S HARD WHEN:	IT'S EASY WHEN:
It's artificial.	It's real and natural.
It's broken into bits and pieces.	It's whole.
It's nonsense.	It's sensible.
It's dull and uninteresting.	It's interesting.
It's irrelevant to the learner.	It's relevant.
It belongs to somebody else.	It belongs to the learner.
It's out of context.	It's part of a real event.
It has no social value.	It has social utility.
It has no discernible purpose.	It has purpose for the learner.
It's imposed by someone else.	The learner chooses to use it.
It's inaccessible.	It's accessible to the learner.
The learner is powerless.	The learner has power to use it.

Figure 3.3 What makes language very easy or very hard to learn? (Goodman, 1986, p. 8)

The activities commonly labeled as the language experience approach (LEA) are based on a three-part premise:

1. Thoughts can be verbalized in oral language.

2. Oral language can be represented in writing.

3. Written language can be read.

The advantage over approaches that start with words and word parts (phonics) is that this approach starts with the learner's own words and experiences. Thus, the learner starts with meaningful language. Once the learner's own oral language can be represented in print, lessons can be developed which focus on meaning (comprehension), on sound-symbol correspondences (phonics), sentence patterns (syntax), punctuation, and word patterns (spelling). This is a very important consideration for English language learners who so often struggle in initial attempts to read because of the irregularities of the sound-symbol system of the English language. Table 3.1 is a summary of student characteristics and corresponding instructional procedures for a language experience program. Students are leveled accord-

Table 3.1 Language Experience Approach Summary Chart for ESL Students (Dixon & Nessel, 1983, pp. 6–7)

	Student Characteristics	Instructional Procedures	Oral Language/ Dictation Topics	Reading-related Activities
Stage 1	Almost no oral English; no experience with any written language	Key vocabulary; dictated pattern stories	Student's daily experience; structured experiences of immediate utility	Conversation; role-playing; listening to stories; word discrimination activities
Stage 2	Some oral English; some fluency with written native language	Story dictation; structured word lists	Student's daily experiences; American cultural events such as holidays or typical family celebrations; other American customs	Read-along books; dramatic reading; word recognition activities
Stage 3	Considerable oral English; fluency in oral and written native language and English	Story dictation; story language revision	Student's daily experiences; new areas of learning such as other academic areas; areas of special interest the student is studying	Rewriting of dictation; developing study skills; responding to literature

ing to degree of mastery of both oral English and written English.

In my own teaching, I have used language experience with both single learners and groups. The technique varies according to the number. If you are working with a single learner, such as in a tutorial setting, have the learner dictate a personal experience. The prompt for this could be a field trip, a story that you have read to the class, or any other series of events that the student has the oral language to describe. As the student dictates the experience, you transcribe it word for word, maintaining the same word order used by the student. Sit next to the student so the student can see what you are writing. Once you have finished the transcription, read it back to the student, making sure the student follows along. After you have done this, have the student read it.

After the student has successfully read the story, you can pick out certain words and structures to work with. Point out words that may have structures similar to other words the student has already learned. Build a sight word bank using the words from the story. These can then be used for future sight word activities, spelling exercises, or future language experience activities.

Even though the language experience approach was originally designed for use with individual learners, it works with groups. In this case, you can have the students take turns dictating each line or sentence of the story. As they do so, you should be prepared to transcribe their words on the board in front of the class or on an overhead transparency projector. Start with an experience that the whole group has shared in class together. This could be a demonstration following a Total Physical Response lesson. Total Physical Response is an approach made popular first in the 1970s in which the teacher acts out a series of commands. The students, in turn, demonstrate comprehension by acting out the verbal command, thus the term Total Physical Response. Initially students are not required to produce language. In this case, have students take turns dictating a step in sequence from the lesson. Again, you transcribe their words as they dictate them. After everyone has contributed, or once the entire sequence of steps has been dictated, you read the steps back to the students.

What about incorrect sentence order or incorrect word usage? My suggestion is to transcribe the language the students dictate, making sure only that the words are correctly spelled. But as a follow-up activity, you can go back with the entire class to make corrections in word and sentence structure. You can then turn your language experience stories into cloze exercises by deleting certain words. You can scramble sentence order to see if they can restore the original sequence. There are many creative applications to a language experience lesson.

Another popular activity used in adult ESL literacy classes for teaching basic level literacy skills is known as the dialogue journal. Dialogue journals allow learners to write about whatever they are interested in or in response to specific prompts from the teacher (Orem, 2001; Peyton & Reed, 1990). The teacher's responsibility is to react (dialogue) with the learner's own dialogue entries, but to avoid correcting the learner's language. An effective teacher can identify errors and develop literacy lessons that focus on those errors commonly committed by the learner. The teacher can provide important feedback either by paraphrasing the learner's own language errors in their responses to the learners, or providing specific prompts to the learner so that the learner gets more practice in using correct form.

Another popular classroom technique in adult literacy classes with conceptual links to whole language is the assessment technique known as the *cloze* procedure. The cloze procedure was first introduced to reading instruction in the 1950s (Taylor, 1953) as a technique for assessing reading difficulty. It derives its name from Gestalt psychology and descriptions of perception. It is considered a holistic assessment technique, as it requires the learner to draw from knowledge of grammar, vocabulary, and background knowledge to make accurate predictions that are required for effective reading comprehension.

To assess the difficulty level of potential reading material, the learner is given an excerpt from the target material with words deleted. Typically, words are randomly deleted (for example, every fifth or seventh word), starting with the second full sentence of the passage. Some proponents advise a text length of at least 250 words

The cloze procedure is generally considered a more accurate assessment of the readability of written text for the English language learner than are conventional readability formulas, such as the Fry Readability Formula (Fry, 1968). These conventional formulas generally rely on quantitative measures such as word length or sentence length on the premise that the longer the word, or the longer the sentence, the more complex, and therefore the more difficult. They do not account for background information or cultural information that the reader has access to which can facilitate comprehension. The cloze procedure, on the other hand, does take background information into account in assessing the level of difficulty of written text. The more background information that the reader can draw from, the more likely the reader will be able to make predictions regarding new information found in the text, and the more likely that the reader will be able to more fully comprehend the written text. Activity 3.1 provides a sample passage with 20 deletions. Read the passage and note your responses.

In the sample passage, I have deleted every seventh word beginning with the second full sentence. A blank space of equal length replaces each missing word. The final sentence is left intact to help provide the reader with additional context clues. You can easily calculate the percentage of accurate responses by multiplying the number of correct responses by 5 (20 possible correct responses × 5 = 100%). You can apply this procedure to a variety of authentic texts as well, such as a newspaper story.

There are no hard-and-fast rules for how to interpret scoring of a cloze procedure. However, Rye (1982) suggests the following guidelines. A correct response rate above 60% would normally indicate that the reader is at the independent level of instruction. That means that the reader could handle this passage with minimal instructional assistance. A correct response rate between 40% and 60% would indicate that the reader is at the instructional level for this passage. That means the reader could understand this passage with some instructional assis-

Activity 3.1
Reading English as a Second Language and the Adult Learner (Bouchard et al., 1974)

Adult students are voluntary learners. They have certain expectations of achievement _____ returning to the classroom. The teacher _____ adults should utilize these students' experiences, _____ adults can respond better if encouraged _____ draw on their personal knowledge. The _____ speaking adult students learning English as _____ second language have several obstacles to _____. Not only must they learn to _____ _____ in a new language, but also _____ must adapt themselves to American culture. _____ on an adult's ability to learn _____ as a second language (ESL) skills _____ aptitude, age, motivation, and native language _____. These influences are variable and can _____ and/or negatively affect ESL learning. Reading _____ as a second language is important _____ order for the non-English adult to _____ effectively and to become more aware _____ himself in relation to his society. _____ factors affect the adult's ability to _____ to read English. They are oral knowledge of English, literacy level in the native language, the native language orthography, and student incentive.

Correct responses: *when, of, because, to, non-English, a, overcome, communicate, they, Influences, English, include, interference, positively, English, in, communicate, of, Several, learn*

tance from the teacher. A correct response rate below 40% would indicate that the reader is probably at a frustration level with this passage. That means that the reader would have difficulty understanding this passage even with instructional assistance from the teacher.

Using the correct or precise word scoring method (fixed-ratio) enables the teacher to score this passage quickly. Using an approximate word scoring method (variable-ratio) allows the teacher to account for reader use of synonyms, or other vocabulary that might still make sense. Even with approximate words, the percentages allowed for the different assessment levels do not change significantly.

The cloze procedure has generated an enormous literature base dating back to Taylor's first discussion of it in *Journalism Quarterly* in 1953. Actually, cloze-type activities had been used in education for many years prior to Taylor. However, Taylor is generally credited with naming the procedure and demonstrating many applications for it (Oller & Jonz, 1994; Rye, 1982). The beauty of this simple technique is that it gauges the interaction of the reader with written text more effectively than other techniques can do.

PERSONAL OBSERVATIONS

Based on what we know from the limited evidence in the field, I can offer some observations of what can work for adult English language learners. First, there is no single model or strategy that will prove effective with all learners. I try to expose my own students to a variety of instructional models so that they are able to make better decisions in the classroom.

Second, adult English language learners who have better developed first language literacy skills together with more years of formal schooling in their first language will tend to acquire second language literacy skills in English faster than those with weaker skills and less experience in formal schooling. Adult English language learners with more developed oral skills in English will tend to acquire literacy skills faster than those adults with weaker oral skills. Oral language development and experience in formal schooling, therefore, appear to be keys to more successful second language literacy development.

Third, adult English language learners need to be good detectives and risk takers. Just as it is important to be a risk taker in oral communication, it is likewise important to take chances when reading. This means guessing at unknown words. Students need to learn from all of the available contextual cues, syntax, punctuation, visuals, anything else that can give clues. This can be a very difficult concept for adult learners who lack confidence in their learning ability. Fourth, adult English language learners, unless they require and don't receive compensation for some form of learning disability (Jordan, 1996), can learn to read. It may be difficult, but as long as their instructor shows patience and support, they can learn.

WHAT SHOULD THE TEACHER DO?

Find relevant material for the learners. Start with what the learners want or need to read. If the learners cannot provide such material, start with what oral language they can produce. Identify key vocabulary in their environment. Help the learners to recognize common sound-symbol correspondences in the language they already know. Help the learners to develop skills at predicting word meaning.

Provide access to reading material in the classroom. Encourage the learners to use the public library. Work with the public library to acquire low-level, high-interest materials in English. If your students are predominantly Spanish-speaking, and if your community is experiencing an increase in its Spanish-speaking population, encourage your local library to acquire Spanish-language books. Again, first language literacy is a great foundation for acquiring second-language literacy.

Help the new reader to be a risk taker. Provide a secure emotional environment within the classroom that allows initiative without fear of losing face.

LEARNING TO WRITE

Learning to write has not received nearly as much attention in adult ESL as learning to speak or read. For years, learning to write was seen as the final stage in language learning, something that would come naturally as the learner learned to speak and read. We know now that effective writing does not occur naturally. It needs to be taught and reinforced throughout the life span (Johnson & Roen, 1989). Little agreement exists as to what elements are most important in teaching writing. Some authorities stress language (syntax, grammar, and vocabulary) and mechanics (spelling and punctuation), some stress content (relevance and originality) and organization (topic and cohesion), while others stress process (getting started and revising) and purpose (audience and reason for writing). Accordingly, a variety of approaches have evolved that attempt to teach writing.

Structural Approaches

These approaches to teaching writing emphasize the structure and mechanics of writing. Based on the assumptions of language teaching inherent in the audiolingual approach, emphasis is on precision rather than originality. Writing is reinforcement for speaking and reading. An example of an exercise using this approach is the controlled composition. The learner is given a model paragraph, for example, and instructed to make a simple change. Perhaps the direction is to change the subject of the paragraph from singular to plural. At a more advanced level it might be to change the tense from present to past. The writer is then expected to make all of the necessary adjustments.

Communicative Approaches

These approaches encourage writers to ask questions and pay attention to audience. Activities tend to be interactive, rather than mechanical. Writing is viewed as purposeful and not an end in itself (Leki, 1992). An example of a writing activity that reflects the communicative approach is the dialogue journal, which I referred to earlier in this chapter. For this activity, the teacher allows a few minutes at the end of each class meeting so that the learner can write personal thoughts or reflections. The teacher collects these journals and engages in a dialogue by writing reactions to the student's thoughts in the margins of the journal. Rather than correcting grammar, punctuation, and spelling, the teacher provides the learner with relevant models of correct language usage in a dialogue format. The journal provides the learner with a level of security not usually found in formal classroom assessment techniques. The teacher can observe problems with the language and develop lesson plans for the class that target these problems.

Participatory Approaches

These approaches flow from a participatory philosophy stressing purpose and social action. Activities are selected according to the lived experiences of the learner. Ideal activities might incorporate action that leads to a sense of empowerment, such as writing letters to local community leaders, businesses, and landlords (Auerbach, 1992). A writing lesson that incorporates a critical approach might start with a discussion of a problem in the lives of the learners. The stimulus for discussion could be a written text, or it could be an object, or a photograph, referred to as *codes* (Gallo, 2004). Newspaper editorial cartoons can provide very meaningful codes for certain local issues. The students engage in a discussion of issues prompted by the codes, and together they develop a written text that becomes the writing activity. The common goal in a participatory classroom is to engage in some form of social action. Good examples of such lessons can be found in Wallerstein (1983) or Nash and others (1992).

Raimes (1983, pp. 12–23) offers seven basic questions that the instructor might want to ask when planning the writing class:

1. How can writing help my students learn their second language better? This is similar to the interaction of reading and learning: At what point does the learner read to learn rather than learn to read?

2. How can I find enough topics? Look to the students for your source of useful topics. What are they interested in?

3. How can I help to make the subject matter meaningful? Start with the lived experiences of your learners.

4. Who will read what my students write? Make sure the learner is aware of who will read what is written. Vary the reader. The teacher shouldn't be the only one to read and respond to the student's writing.

5. How are the students going to work together in the classroom? Just as you would group students in oral language activities, also consider different groupings in writing activities.

6. How much time should I give my students for their writing? This will vary depending on the number of students in the class and the amount of time available for instruction. Always set aside a few minutes of each instructional period for a little writing practice. Try to incorporate writing into all class activities.

7. What do I do about errors? What can we learn from our errors? Help learners to develop a positive attitude toward error correction. Overcorrection can be particularly discouraging for adult learners. Peer correction can be useful at a point when learners begin to show competence and confidence in their skills.

Techniques for Teaching Reading and Writing in the Literacy Classroom

After you have struggled to answer the above questions, it is time to start identifying activities for teaching literacy skills and organizing them into coherent lessons. Here are some techniques that you could try in your classrooms.

1. Use lots of visuals. A picture *IS* worth a thousand words. Take advantage of it. Pictures can provide a group of students

with a common language experience that can generate conversation, written work, and reading exercises.

2. Use authentic materials. The term in the language teaching literature used to describe authentic, tangible material is *realia*. Students can touch them, describe them, and talk about them as they relate to their lives. Rather than bringing to the class pictures of food items, bring the real thing. Teachers in participatory literacy programs might refer to realia as tools. Tools help to make concrete important themes that are relevant to your students.

3. Try read alouds. Reading aloud is a common activity with children. They love to be read to. Adult English language learners also enjoy hearing the spoken word. It reinforces the sounds and structures of the language they so much desire to learn themselves. Try reading aloud a passage while your students have their books closed. Then read it again with books opened.

4. Perform skits. Assign roles to students. Following the skit students can write a summary of what occurred, or write what might happen next.

5. Conduct dictation. Carefully done, a dictation can be an effective way of developing good listening skills while reinforcing writing in a highly structured way. Dictation can also be part of an effective assessment program for listening and writing skill development.

6. Practice letter writing. This activity can be an effective way of teaching adult English language learners about the benefits of living in a democracy. Have the students identify a problem they have experienced in their community. It could be a problem at work, at school, about housing, transportation, or much more. It should be a problem that requires a form of conflict resolution through reasoned discourse. Show your students how a letter can be structured to effectively communicate with a government representative, a school official,

a community leader, the newspaper, a local business. See what happens after the letters are mailed.

SUMMARY

Literacy has become a critical component of programs of instruction for adult English language learners. There are many ways to approach literacy instruction, based on your definition of what literacy is. Three early influences on my emerging understanding of literacy include competency-based programs that followed the Adult Performance Level Study of 1977, the participatory approach to literacy originally articulated by Paulo Freire, and the whole language theories of literacy that were first articulated by Frank Smith, and later Ken Goodman and others. Each of these approaches rests on very different theoretical bases and philosophical assumptions of what reading is and why literacy is critical for adult learners.

These three approaches also underlie much of writing instruction, including the more mechanical assumptions of controlled composition, the communicative assumptions of dialogue journals, and the social-action-oriented assumptions inherent in Freirian literacy classrooms. As a literacy teacher, or an administrator of a literacy program, you will make curricular and instructional decisions based on your understanding of the nature of literacy and the purposes for literacy that guide the learners in your program.

CHAPTER 4

Organizing Instruction

Most adult ESL teachers have a limited role in program building within the larger context of the education provider, whether that be a community college, a public school system, a faith-based or community-based organization, a volunteer organization, or a business. However, it is also fair to say that adult ESL teachers should be knowledgeable of program components, because they may find themselves in a position of developing a program for a community organization, or serving on a team that will seek to improve the program they already work for.

In addition to considering the different types of program providers, it is important to consider some of the basic and most common types of instructional programs designed for adult English language learners (National Center for ESL Literacy Education, 2003). These programs include those that provide general, or survival, English language skills. Such programs are most common and employ the vast majority of adult ESL teachers. Another type of program is the family literacy program. These programs are designed to teach parents and children together. Such programs are particularly appealing to parents of pre-school-age children. The usual mission of such programs is to break the cycle of illiteracy in families by targeting the language needs of both children and caregivers. Another type of program that has received a great deal of attention in the last several years is the program that focuses on civics education. Such programs target new immigrants who are interested in becoming citizens of the United States. In addition to citizenship, these programs also teach English language learners about their civil rights. These programs gained popularity after passage of the 1986 Immigration Reform and Control Act (PL 99–603), amnesty legislation that enabled many heretofore undocumented workers to apply for citizenship.

The remaining two program types focus on job-related language skills. The reauthorized Workforce Investment Act of 1998 put a special emphasis on instruction that would lead to employment. One of these programs, called vocational ESL, instructs English language learners about general vocational-related skills, such as job interviewing and expected behaviors for work. Enrolled learners in these programs may or may not already be employed. The final type of program can be called workplace ESL. These programs are offered in the workplace, the learners are all employees together in that workplace, and the language of instruction focuses on the language used in that workplace.

There are certainly other ways to define the goals of adult English language programs. In addition to the orientations listed above, you can also find programs that build instruction around topics of personal relevance to the learner and topics that focus on social change (Wrigley & Guth, 1992). These curricula aren't as widely seen as the others because they tend not to be favored by the major funders, primarily federal and state agencies. You might more likely find these two orientations within programs that are community-based or volunteer-driven.

With all of these approaches to program design, it is important to take note of how general principles of adult education have influenced the practice of organizing instruction, regardless of context (National Center for ESL Literacy Educaton, 2003). These planning principles are based on:

1. Knowledge of adult learning and adult second language acquisition.

2. Teaching techniques that are responsive to learning styles, needs and goals, and an awareness of learning disabilities.

3. Assessment of learners' needs and goals that is ongoing and authentic.

4. Content that draws from learners' prior experiences.

5. Content that is relevant and immediately usable to the learner.

6. Involvement of learners in planning.

7. Course intensity and duration designed to fit learners' needs.
   (p. 13)

In spite of the development of these effective instructional practices, adult ESL programs still struggle to effectively reach all of those learners that may qualify for instruction. Among the barriers to more effective instruction are the increasing numbers of immigrants that often overwhelm the capacities of local programs, inadequate funding, and the difficulty in finding qualified instructors. For the purposes of discussion, I define qualified instructors as those who have had some formal training in teaching English as a second language culminating in a degree or certificate.

What follows in this chapter is a discussion of some of the basic components of programs designed for adult English language learners. I will start with a discussion of goal setting and mission. I will then compare two major curricular approaches: what I call the conventional approach and the participatory approach.

GOAL SETTING AND MISSION

Most adult ESL programs are housed within larger organizational frameworks that already have a mission statement. It is important that the adult ESL program also fit within that larger framework and be compatible with the mission statement of the parent organization.

Few programs will be unable to furnish a mission statement, as funding agencies have become more insistent on them. Mission statements reflect general program philosophy within the context of the larger institution. Mission statements should help to frame the general parameters of the institution or curriculum and should also reveal that program's core values. The following points were taken from a mission statement developed for a community college.

- Provide quality educational programs and services which are academically, geographically, financially, technologically, and physically accessible to meet the educational and training needs of a diverse, multicultural population and the organizations within its community.
- Maintain institutional policies, programs, practices, and efforts which provide an emphasis on a learning-centered college for students and the community.
- Commit to the intellectual, physical, social, cultural, and career development of the individual.
- Promote diversity in faculty, staff, and student recruitment; staff development; curriculum development; and cultural enrichment activities.
- Contribute to the economic, workforce, social, recreational, and cultural quality of life of the community.
- Cooperate with other local, state and national organizations and provide leadership that will enhance educational services and avoid duplication of services. (Available from www.waubonsee.edu/about/mission.php)

TESOL's *Standards for Adult Education ESL Programs* (TESOL, 2003) starts with a discussion of Standards for Program Structure, Administration, and Planning. The first statement within this section is as follows: "The program has a mission statement, a clearly articulated philosophy, and goals developed with input from internal and external stakeholders" (p. 19). Internal stakeholders could include staff and students. External stakeholders could include funding agencies and community members, such as social service agencies, and potential and actual employers of graduates from these programs.

Program administrators are frequently asked to review program goals and mission. It wouldn't hurt to also involve instructors in this effort. Take the time, too, to visit other programs and find out what they are doing that may be unique, or that you may be able to adapt to your program (Activity 4.1).

Activity 4.1
The Adult ESL Program Practitioner Interview

Visit an adult ESL program for the purpose of interviewing the director or other staff member in a position to provide answers to the following questions:

1. Does the program have an underlying rationale (mission statement)? Is it stated in the curriculum guide or elsewhere, or is it merely implied?

2. How does the operation of the program conform to the stated (or implied) mission? Give specific examples.

3. Has the program engaged in any form of self-study or program evaluation within the past five years? If so, what did the program learn from this activity?

4. How does this program recruit its students? How does it otherwise promote itself?

5. How are student needs assessed? How are students placed in different levels of instruction? How is student progress or achievement assessed?

6. How many staff are employed by this program? What special qualifications do these staff members bring to their work?

7. What are, in your opinion, the unique features of this program?

8. Is the curriculum used in this program participatory? Conventional? What model does it most closely reflect (general survival language, family literacy, vocational, etc.)?

9. What is your overall impression of this program? Imagine you were the director of this program. What would you do to change any aspect of this program to improve its functioning?

COMPARING CURRICULAR APPROACHES

Although an examination of different programs for adult English language learners may reveal some nuances in curricular approaches, I will focus here on two major approaches: the conventional approach and the participatory approach. The conventional approach is represented by descriptions offered by Brown (1995) and Richards (2001). The participatory approach is well represented through the writings of Auerbach (1992) and Smoke (1998) and Wallerstein (1983). Nunan (1988) has contributed his ideas of learner-centered curriculum development, but does not include the element of social change that is so important to participatory approaches. Figure 4.1 will help to organize a comparative analysis of these two types.

Needs

All program planning begins with some form of needs assessment. The difference between conventional and participatory approaches is that conventional approaches tend to derive needs from the external environment, whereas a participatory approach sees needs as emanating from the lived experiences of the learner. Actually, participatory educators are even reluctant to use the term *need* as it may imply some deficit on the part of the learner. In a participatory program, learners are viewed as knowledge "producers," not knowledge "consumers." Therefore, an assessment of need is actually an assessment of what knowledge the learner already has and how the learner is able to relate to new knowledge.

Content

Conventional approaches present the learner with predetermined goals and objectives that, in turn, help to determine the content of instruction. These goals and objectives are often determined by program mission, the larger institution's mis-

CONVENTIONAL APPROACH	PARTICIPATORY APPROACH
Focus	**Focus**
Focus on language; traditional ends-means approach; driven by external stakeholders.	Focus on action; emergent curriculum; driven by needs of internal stakeholders (learners).
Needs analysis	**Needs assessment**
Based on a deficit model; needs are determined by external stakeholders.	Determined by learner; focus is on problems in immediate social context.
Goals and objectives	**Determining content**
Determined by external stakeholders.	Learners work together with teachers to determine content.
Testing	**Assessment**
Characterized by standardized tests; need to compare outcomes with other programs; results are commonly quantitative.	Authentic, ongoing, qualitative, informal, learner-centered.
Materials	**Materials**
Reliance on commercial materials; calibrated to testing program.	Authentic; student-generated; draws from local resources.
Teaching	**Teaching and learning**
Teacher is primary authority.	Learner-centered; teacher is a co-learner.
Program evaluation	**Determining outcomes**
Accomplishment of outcomes determined by external stakeholders.	Success determined not only by individual achievement but by improvements in local community and increased empowerment of learners.

Figure 4.1 Comparing curricular approaches

sion, and, perhaps most importantly, the mission of the funding agency. Since most adult ESL is funded by federal and state tax dollars, content is most often shaped in terms of economic needs of the community. Participatory programs, on the other hand, determine content by the actual goals of the learner. These goals are stated in terms of social change and personal empowerment. Language may provide the core content in a conventional curriculum, whereas language is seen as a means to a greater end in a participatory curriculum.

Testing and Assessment

Assessment has become a focus of the national discussion on education at all levels. Testing and assessment are tied to accountability of programs and learners. Testing here refers to a measure of achievement at a point in time and is determined by means of both informal and formal (standardized) instruments. Assessment refers to a more holistic measure of progress toward student goals and includes a variety of indicators that may make up a student portfolio (Van Duzer & Berdan, 2000). Federally funded adult ESL programs require testing of students to determine progress toward specified ends. According to the National Reporting System for Adult Education (NRS) (2001), "state and local programs may use any assessment procedures desired, as long as the procedures are standardized for all programs in the same way" (p. 19). The reason usually given for use of standardized tests is to be able to compare students across programs in order to provide an indication of program quality and to provide statewide data that can be used both to reward high performing and to sanction low performing programs. The language of the NRS suggests that states may use a standardized instrument, such as the Basic English Skills Test (BEST, n.d.) or the Comprehensive Adult Standard Assessment System (CASAS) Assessment of Life Skills tests (CASAS, n.d.). A number of states have chosen this option. Other states are developing their own systems, which are allowed so long as the assessment tools and their descriptors are compatible with NRS levels and skills.

The National Reporting System for Adult Education was formally instituted in 1997. It was a response to the criticism shared by some legislators in Congress that there was no nation-wide uniform system for collecting data on student progress that could link achievement in basic reading and writing with acquisition of workplace skills. The NRS identifies five core outcome measures that address the requirements of the Adult Education and Family Literacy Act for core performance indicators: educational gain; employment; employment retention; placement in postsecondary education or training; and receipt of a secondary education or training.

Of course, such a system is not without its critics. Some would argue that this system places far too much emphasis on interpreting success using quantitative data, primarily test scores. It ignores all of those other measures of success such as improved healthcare or ability to deal more successfully with a child's homework. Appendix A provides the National Reporting System ESL functioning level descriptors and their benchmarks with assorted standardized measures.

The National Reporting System model provides a six-level assessment tool starting with beginning ESL literacy and moving to high advanced ESL. Together with these six levels are four categories of content and assessment benchmarks that describe the characteristics of the English language learner at each level. Beginning ESL literacy is characterized as a general absence of ability to communicate in English. High advanced ESL students are described as having the ability to use oral and written English effectively, but not necessarily at the level of an educated native speaker. They are capable of meeting most workplace requirements and are in a position to pursue self-directed learning as needed.

Benchmarks refer to speaking, reading, and writing instruments commonly used in adult ESL programs. As mentioned above, the CASAS, Oral BEST, Literacy BEST, and BEST Plus are all standardized instruments. Student Performance Levels (SPL) were developed as part of the Mainstream English Language Project (MELT) to describe communication abilities at 10 different levels and were used in assessment of language progress made by refugees in resettlement and cultural orientation programs in the 1980s. SPL descriptions are found in Appendix B.

Authentic Assessment

Authentic assessment offers a sharp contrast to standardized testing. Whereas standardized testing looks at the learner at one point in time in relation to criteria that are determined external to the learner, authentic assessment makes the attempt to look at the learner's progress over time and according to criteria that are directly related to the learner's own goals. Common activities associated with authentic assessment include language and literacy inventories, reading and writing samples, and informal interviews, all of which might be contained in a portfolio.

Auerbach (1992) offers a set of guiding principles that characterize authentic, or "alternative" assessment in the context of participatory programs. Authentic evaluation is:

- Contextualized, context-specific, and variable; assessment is situated in real-life contexts using actions that replicate the real life needs of the learner.
- Qualitative; assessment attempts to measure the complexity of language rather than reduce it to abstract numbers.
- Process-oriented; assessment is interested in answers to questions of how and why, rather than focusing only on end results.
- Ongoing and integrated with instruction; assessment occurs concurrently with instruction.
- Supportive; assessment focuses on what students can do, rather than what they can't do.
- Done with students, not to them; assessment is done in students' best interests, rather than to report to an external funder to compare program effectiveness.
- Two-way; in addition to assessing their own progress, students also engage in program evaluation.

TRADITIONAL ASSESSMENT	ALTERNATIVE ASSESSMENT
One-shot, standardized exams	Continuous long-term assessment
Timed, multiple-choice format	Untimed, free-response format
Decontextualized test items	Contextualized communicative tasks
Scores suffice for feedback	Individualized feedback and washback
Norm-referenced scores	Criterion-referenced scores
Focus on the "right" answer	Open-ended, creative answers
Summative	Formative
Oriented to product	Oriented to process
Non-interactive performance	Interactive performance
Fosters extrinsic motivation	Fosters intrinsic motivation

Figure 4.2 Traditional and alternative assessment (Brown, 2004, p. 13)

- Open-ended; assessment allows for unexpected outcomes, and is not limited to pre-determined objectives. (p. 114)

Brown (2004) summarizes some of the major distinctions between "traditional" and "alternative" assessment in Figure 4.2. He cautions the reader that these are "overgeneralizations and should therefore be considered with caution" (p. 13), but I believe they are distinctions held by a majority of those who have been working in the field as teachers, curriculum writers, and staff developers. As stated, these descriptions favor alternative assessment. Both forms of assessment have a role in the overall scheme of instruction and measurement of learner progress. However, because of the common working conditions facing adult ESL instructors, and because of the very nature of the adult

English language learner, I encourage teachers to become familiar with the strategies that are labeled alternative assessment, because they provide the ongoing feedback to the teacher that is so important when making day-by-day decisions about what to teach.

Materials

Conventional programs rely heavily on published materials that are language-based. More highly qualified teachers are often able to supplement commercial materials with high quality materials of their own. Participatory programs may make some use of commercial materials, but tend to draw more heavily on authentic materials, those materials that actually come from the students' work and family environments. A participatory classroom, for example, might start with an item brought to class by a student. This item somehow represents an aspect of that student's environment that may be seen as a challenge or barrier to quality of life. In other words, materials in a participatory program tend to carry a value that evokes a strong emotional response on the part of the learner. Materials in conventional programs more frequently are seen as neutral, or at least as avoiding conflict.

Wrigley and Guth (1992) provide teachers and administrators a thorough list of questions to help guide their decision making. These questions are clustered in categories labeled need; linking ESL literacy to program focus, language and literacy; linking text to student needs, goals, and experiences; expanding the students' background knowledge, cultural bias; linking teacher experience and interest with the materials, print accessibility, adaptability, and assessment (pp. 47–51). All of this can be summarized in general guidelines they offer by saying "Much depends on the approach a program supports, the preference of learners and teachers, the availability of commercial materials suitable for the program's purposes, and the time, money, interest, and experience available to develop program-based materials" (pp. 46–47).

Teaching and Learning

Conventional programs of instruction tend to emphasize teaching. Participatory programs tend to emphasize learning. This is obviously an oversimplification of a complex transaction that goes on every day in adult ESL programs. But the distinction is an important one and reflects values that are espoused throughout the adult education literature. Because a great majority of adult ESL teachers have had little exposure to methods and materials of teaching adults, let alone to teaching adult English language learners, the limited staff development they do receive tends to focus on specific techniques they can use "tomorrow" or "Monday." In other words, they seek immediate solutions in the form of activities that can help their adult students learn. However, in participatory programs, instructors are viewed more as facilitators or co-learners. Learners have greater input into the content and objectives of the program. The concepts of learning community and community of learners are more frequently used concepts within a participatory program.

Program Evaluation and Determining Outcomes

Program evaluation is an important aspect of accountability for conventional programs. This is most often due to requirements of funding agencies. Effective program evaluation feeds back into the program planning process by identifying new needs for internal and external stakeholders, as well as effectiveness in how the program meets current goals and objectives. Participatory programs, by nature of the process by which learners help shape the curriculum, may evaluate program effectiveness simply in terms of how learners are able to effect change in their environments as a result of having participated in the program. Participatory programs are often not funded by external agencies, but are most frequently found in community-based organizations in the United States and Canada. Regardless of funding source, educators in a truly participatory program would have to insist on complete control of how outcomes are determined and are unlikely to rely on traditional measures of progress found in conventional programs. Whereas success in a conventional program might mean good test scores on a standardized instrument, or job placement in the local community as a result of improved language skills, success in a participatory program might mean the formation of a local tenants association that fights to improve living conditions for migrant workers in the community.

SUMMARY

In this chapter we look at the elements of planning and administering programs of instruction for adult English language learners. We start with a discussion of mission and program objectives. Then we move to a comparison of curricular approaches that looks specifically at learner needs, curricular content, assessment, materials, teaching process, and program evaluation. Each of these elements is treated differently depending on program philosophy. Most programs for teaching adult English language learners use a conventional approach to program design. Here objectives are determined external to the learner's personal context and the learner remains uninvolved in all of the major decisions affecting instruction and assessment. This conventional approach is contrasted with a more participatory approach in which all phases of program planning involve the learner as a partner with teachers and administrators. In the next chapter, you will be introduced to methods of teaching cross-cultural skills to adult English language learners. Culture and language are seen as indelibly linked in the process of becoming proficient in a second language.

CHAPTER 5

Teaching Cross-Cultural Skills

During my doctoral studies at the University of Georgia I worked part-time as an adult literacy and ESL instructor for the local adult basic education program. One of the classes I taught was a basic level adult literacy class. The students were young and old, male and female, black and white. They came to the program with various reasons for why they wanted to learn to read and write.

Marlene was a doctoral student in the reading program at the university. Like me, Marlene was not originally from the South. She volunteered to assist me in my class so that she could have experience working with adult nonreaders. She came to the class early that Monday evening. I spoke with her about some of the students, their problems and aspirations. We went over the materials and agreed that she would do some one-on-one tutoring with Jessie, one of my lowest level readers, an African-American woman in her 50s who worked days as a domestic for some of the local families in town and whose main goal was to read the Bible on her own and to read to her grandchildren.

At the end of that first evening session, after all of the students had left, Marlene sighed, "I feel so middle class!" "Middle class," I thought. Was it simply coincidence that she should say that? After all, I had been toying with the same idea for my dissertation for several months. Not only how does culture influence learning, but also how does culture influence teaching? More specifically, given the fact that the majority of basic literacy teachers come from middle class and middle income families, and our students come overwhelmingly from working class and lower income families, does our cultural background influence

at all how we approach our own teaching in the adult basic edu-
cation classroom? This concept had first come to me as a Peace
Corps volunteer teaching English to adults in Tunis, and was
later reinforced when I taught at Henry McNeal Turner High
School in Atlanta, Georgia, an all-black high school in the initial
stages of court-ordered desegregation. Interestingly, the only per-
sonnel in that school that was integrated was the teaching staff,
not the students. And it appeared that the white teachers had a
lot to learn about working with a student population with whom
they had little cultural experience in common.

It is often said that you can't learn a second language effectively without also understanding the culture of those who
speak the target language. I think that describes my experience
well, not only as a literacy teacher, but also as a teacher of English as a foreign language. The metaphor of the iceberg is appropriate here. What many people think represents culture is
only that 10% that appears above the water line. This would
include the institutions with which we govern, and through
which we educate, our literature, the arts, our food. In short,
all of those visible qualities that define who we are. However,
when I speak of culture in my classes, I am referring to that 90%
that lies below the water line. This refers to those underlying
values and assumptions that shape how we think and speak,
how we interact verbally and nonverbally, and how we view the
larger world in which we live and work.

I have to admit that prior to beginning my work in Tunisia,
my initial exposure to Arabic and the Arab culture was not too
positive. All of our news from the Middle East is filtered through
a very few news outlets. The only information I had been exposed to from that part of the world was shaped by the American press and government. And in the late 1960s, the picture of
the Arab world for most Americans was not a positive one, not
unlike that picture 40 years later. My initial response to learning
Arabic was that I considered it to be a relatively unattractive
sounding language, compared to what I had grown accustomed
to in French and Italian.

But within weeks of immersing myself in the local Tunisian

culture, I began to feel real progress toward my primary goal of understanding my new host culture. The Peace Corps has a term for this, "going native." I was determined to learn as much as I could about this language and culture, about which I had so little knowledge. What is even more remarkable is that the more I learned about the culture, the more positively I felt about it, and the more progress I made in the language. And as I learned more about the language and culture, I began to understand the world view of my hosts. Benjamin Whorf (1956) was one of the first to put this phenomenon into words. According to Whorf,

> The background linguistic system (in other words, the grammar) of each language is not merely a reproducing instrument for voicing ideas but rather is itself the shaper of ideas, the program and guide for the individual's mental activity, for his analysis of impressions, for his synthesis of his mental stock in trade. Formulation of ideas is not an independent process, strictly rational in the old sense, but is part of a particular grammar, and differs, from slightly to greatly, between different grammars. (pp. 212–13)

This theory of linguistic relativity simply states that the language we speak is a great influence on how we think. It provides the vocabulary and the organization for how we view our world. This concept was later reinforced by the Russian psychologist Lev Vygotsky (1986) who likewise viewed language and thought as influenced by our sociocultural experience. Anyone who has learned to speak another language can quickly see how language reflects the way we see the world around us. English reflects the dynamism of a technological world. Its ability to adapt to its environment makes it difficult to learn for those who come from a language that values regularity. Arabic reflects the integration of a religious belief system into the everyday lives of those who speak the language. Learning Arabic requires learning about the major religious beliefs of the people who speak that language.

It also goes without saying that to optimize your effectiveness as a teacher of adult English language learners two things need to occur. First, as a teacher you need to have a positive attitude toward the learner and toward that learner's home language and culture. The second thing is that the learners need to think positively about the language they are learning. They need to be motivated by a desire to learn, and a belief in themselves that they can learn. There is a definite affective dimension to second language teaching and learning. The learners must feel a connection to the teacher and the teacher needs to be supportive of the learners.

DIMENSIONS OF CULTURE

How is culture reflected in our behaviors and attitudes in the classroom and in the larger world where our students live? Are there universal values held by different cultures that affect how members of those cultures behave and interact toward others? Let's first consider the American culture. Imagine you are in another country and are talking to a group of people who are planning to visit the United States for the very first time. Your task is to provide an orientation to American culture, to prepare these visitors for what they are going to find when they visit and attempt to interact with Americans. What are you going to say? Are Americans friendly toward strangers? Do Americans prefer to spend time with others or do they tend to prefer being left alone? Are they workaholics or do they like to enjoy their time away from their jobs?

The danger we face when listing these broad generalizations is drifting into simple stereotypes of American culture. Americans are materialistic (their economy is driven by consumer spending) and individualistic (the individual comes before the group). They are generous (they give a lot of money to charitable causes) and religious (nearly 90% say they believe in God). Of course, all of these characteristics are true of some Americans, maybe even most Americans. But they aren't necessarily true of all Americans.

Hofstede (2001) provides us a thoroughly researched view of culture as it relates to our values and everyday behaviors. He drew his findings from surveys of tens of thousands of employees of one multinational corporation with offices in over 50 countries throughout the world. From his surveys he developed a theoretical framework for examining culture as it influences interactions in the workplace, in the family, and in the classroom. Hofstede argues that members of any society act according to "mental programs that are developed in the family in early childhood and reinforced in schools and organizations, and that these mental programs contain a component of national culture." (p. xix) The five dimensions that he eventually identified as a way of examining cross-cultural interactions are power distance (low to high), uncertainty avoidance (low to high), individualism versus collectivism, masculinity versus femininity, and time orientation (long and short). Following are definitions of each of these dimensions followed by behaviors or values that may be evident in the classroom.

Power Distance

Power distance is the extent to which the less powerful members of organizations and institutions accept and expect that power is distributed unequally. The basic problem involved is the degree of human inequality that underlies the functioning of each particular society. Figure 5.1 provides some characteristics of teachers and students as found by Hofstede (2001, p. 107) in low and high power distance societies.
Which statements characterize most teachers in American classrooms? Do you see these characteristics manifested in your own classes? Do these characteristics help to explain the discomforts expressed by some English language learners?

Uncertainty Avoidance

Uncertainty avoidance is the extent to which a culture programs its members to feel either uncomfortable or comfortable in unstructured situations. Unstructured situations are novel, unknown, surprising, and different from usual. The basic prob-

LOW POWER DISTANCE INDEX	HIGH POWER DISTANCE INDEX
Teachers treat students as equals.	Students depend on teachers.
Students treat teachers as equals.	Students treat teachers with respect, even outside class.
Student-centered education.	Teacher-centered education.
Students initiate some communication in class.	Teachers initiate all communication in class.
Teachers are experts who transfer impersonal truths.	Teachers are gurus who transfer personal wisdom.
Quality of learning depends on two-way communication and excellence of students.	Quality of learning depends on excellence of teachers.
Lower educational levels maintain more authoritarian relations.	Authoritarian values are independent of education levels.
More modest expectations on benefits of technology.	High expectations on benefits of technology.

Figure 5.1 Key differences between low and high power societies in schools

lem involved is the degree to which a society tries to control the uncontrollable. Figure 5.2 provides some characteristics of classrooms in societies that score low or high on the uncertainty-avoidance index (Hofstede, 2001, p. 169).

Which statements characterize most teachers in American classrooms? Do you see these characteristics manifested in your own classes? Do you recognize characteristics of adult English language learners from certain countries? Do these characteristics help to explain the discomforts expressed by some adult learners?

LOW UNCERTAINTY AVOIDANCE	HIGH UNCERTAINTY AVOIDANCE
Students expect open-ended learning situations and good discussions.	Students expect structured learning situations and seek right answers.
Teachers may say, "I don't know."	Teachers supposed to have all answers.
Students learn that truth may be relative.	Students learn that Truth is absolute.
Students attribute achievements to own ability.	Students attribute achievements to effort, context, and luck.
Dialect speech positively valued.	Dialect speech negatively valued.
Independence for female students important.	Traditional role models for female students.

Figure 5.2 Key characteristics of low and high uncertainty avoidance societies in the classroom

Individualism and Collectivism

Individualism on the one side versus its opposite, collectivism, is the degree to which individuals are supposed to look after themselves or remain integrated into groups, usually around the family. Positioning between these poles is a very basic problem all societies face. Figure 5.3 reports some of Hofstede's (2001, p. 236) findings related to teacher and student dominant roles in both collective and individualist societies.

Which statements characterize most teachers in American classrooms? Do you see these characteristics manifested in your own classes? Do you recognize characteristics of adult English language learners from certain countries? Do these characteristics help to explain the discomforts expressed by some adult learners?

COLLECTIVIST SOCIETIES	INDIVIDUALIST SOCIETIES
Teachers deal with students as a group.	Teachers deal with individual students.
Students' individual initiatives discouraged.	Students' individual initiatives encouraged.
Students report ethnocentric, traditional views.	Students report "modern" views.
Students associate according to preexisting in-group ties.	Students associate according to tasks and current needs.
Students expect preferential treatment by teachers from their in-group.	In-group membership is no reason to expect preferential treatment.
Harmony, face, and shaming in class.	Students' selves to be respected.
Students will not speak up in class or large groups.	Students expected to speak up in class or large groups.
Students' aggressive behavior bad for academic performance.	Students' self-esteem good for academic performance.
Purpose of education is learning how to do.	Purpose of education is learning how to learn.
Diplomas provide entry to higher-status groups.	Diplomas increase economic worth and/or self-respect.

Figure 5.3 Key differences between collectivist and individualist societies in schools

Masculinity and Femininity

Masculinity, and its opposite, femininity, refer to the distribution of emotional roles between the genders, which is another fundamental problem for any society to which a range of solutions are found; it opposes "tough" masculine to "tender"

feminine societies. Figure 5.4 provides a summary of key characteristics that Hofstede (2001, p. 306) used to characterize
teacher and student behaviors along this dimension.

Which statements characterize most teachers in American classrooms? Do you see these characteristics manifested in your own
classes? Do you recognize characteristics of adult English language learners from certain countries? Do these characteristics help to explain the discomforts expressed by some adult
learners?

Time Orientation

Long-term versus short-term orientation refers to the extent to which a culture programs its members to accept delayed
gratification of their material, social, and emotional needs. This
last dimension was not included in Hofstede's earlier studies and
actually resulted from suggestions by Chinese scholars and incorporated into a different instrument, the Chinese Value Survey, developed by another cross-cultural researcher, Michael
Harris Bond, of the Chinese University of Hong Kong. This survey was administered in only 23 countries. Figure 5.5 provides
several key characteristics of students and teachers from both
short-term and long-term orientation societies (Hofstede, 2001,
p. 366).

Which statements characterize most teachers in American
classrooms? Do you see these characteristics manifested in your
own classes? Do you recognize characteristics of adult English
language learners from certain countries? Do these characteristics help to explain the discomforts expressed by some adult
learners?

Where Do You Fit in Hofstede's Framework?

According to Hofstede's findings, most Americans in his
response group score high in individualism (first among all
countries represented), relatively low in power distance (38th
among 50 countries in the response group), low in uncertainty

MORE FEMININE	MORE MASCULINE
Friendliness in teachers appreciated.	Brilliance in teachers appreciated.
Students' social adaptation important.	Students' performance important.
Failing in school is a minor accident.	Failing in school is a disaster.
Public praise to encourage weak students.	Public praise to reward good students.
No special awards.	Awards for good students, teachers.
Average student is the norm.	Best student is the norm.
Curriculum choices guided by intrinsic interest.	Curriculum choices guided by career expectations.
Children socialized to avoid aggression.	Children socialized to fight back.
Students take own problems less seriously.	Own problems taken very seriously.
Ego effacing: own performance underrated.	Ego boosting: performance overrated.
Foreign students in U.S. efface national ego.	Foreign students in U.S. boost national ego.
Young children taught by men and women.	Young children taught by women only.
Teachers give equal attention to girls and boys.	Teachers pay more attention to boys.
Small gender difference in perceptual abilities.	Large differences in perceptual ability: boys analytic, girls contextual.

Figure 5.4 Key differences between feminine and masculine societies in schools

SHORT-TERM ORIENTATION	LONG-TERM ORIENTATION
Quick results expected.	Persistence, perseverance.
Status not a major issue in relationships.	Relationships ordered by status and this order observed.
Respect for traditions.	Adaptation of traditions to new circumstances.
Children should learn tolerance and respect for other people.	Children should learn thrift.
Students consider "persistent" not an important personality trait.	Students consider "persistent" an important personality trait.
Most important events in life occurred in past or occur in present.	Most important events in life will occur in future.

Figure 5.5 Key differences between short- and long-term-oriented societies

avoidance (43rd among 50 countries studied), and relatively higher on the masculinity index (15th among 50 countries studied). Finally, the United States scores in the lower half of the 23 countries on the long-term orientation index, indicating a preference for short-term orientation. Other countries consistently scoring nearly the same as the United States on most indices include Canada, New Zealand, Australia, and the Netherlands.

For comparison's sake, I offer the relative position of Mexico, the source of a great number of students in our adult ESL programs. Mexico ranks relatively high on the power distance index (tied for 5th place among 50 countries with Venezuela), low on the individualism index (32nd among 50 countries), high on the uncertainty avoidance index (18th among 50 countries), and high on the masculinity index (6th place). Mexico was not included in countries scored on long-term orientation.

The contrast between the United States and Mexico in this analysis is stark. According to Hofstede's findings, most educational institutions in Mexico would be teacher-centered (high power distance). Teachers are respected as the sole authority and are not to be questioned (high uncertainty avoidance). Individual initiative is discouraged (collectivistic). Male and female roles are traditionally defined (masculine). The implication for adult ESL teachers is that we can expect that students of Mexican origin enter our classrooms in the United States with preconceived notions of how to behave as students that are diametrically opposed to the values and norms of the typical American classroom and classroom teacher. This is made even more dramatic by the fact that a significant percentage of Mexican-origin adult ESL learners have very limited experiences in formal schooling. These are also the ones with the greatest need for skilled instructors.

Since many adult English language learners seek to become somewhat assimilated into mainstream American culture, it makes sense that they will want to adapt to the cultural values of the dominant group. However, their own values have been learned over a lifetime of experiences and cannot be simply forgotten. After all, every culture has its own set of rules that define the behavior and values of that culture. To acknowledge that another culture has equally valid behaviors based on equally valid assumptions about the world can be viewed as a threat to the learner's core values. When this happens, the learner experiences culture shock. The teacher often becomes the one to help the learner pass through this phase of the acculturation cycle.

What does it take to be successful in a new culture? Many people have attempted to answer this question. Just think how helpful you could be with your own learners if you knew the answer to this question. There have been many attempts to find out what conditions lead to success in cross-cultural adaptation. I have discovered one commercial product that may help you to begin your own analysis of the factors that lead to successful cross-cultural adaptation. It is the Cross-Cultural Adaptability

Inventory (CCAI™), developed by Colleen Kelley and Judith Meyers (1993). This is a self-scoring assessment that can help teachers identify personal strengths and weaknesses in four areas deemed important for successful cross-cultural adaptation. I would recommend use of this instrument as a staff development activity to generate discussion and reflection about the topic of cross-cultural adaptability with implications for your adult learners as well. For more information about this instrument, contact Pearson Assessments at 1-800-627-7271, ext. 3225, or 1-925-681-3225. Visit them online at www.pearsonassessments. com/test/ccai.htm.

To better understand the potential conflicts that may be grounded in the differing value systems found in different cultures, try the Cross-Cultural Analysis in Activity 5.1. I have been using this informal instrument for years with my graduate students and have suggested it as a staff development activity for adult ESL programs. An early version of this activity was given to me by a colleague over 25 years ago to be used as an informal self-assessment tool. Its original source is unknown. I have since modified it, but a close look reveals that the items are designed to stimulate discussion about many of the key characteristics that are often used to stereotype Americans.

The cross-cultural analysis activity can be effective with both teachers and administrators. As such, it is an easy-to-use staff development and community building exercise. Simply follow the directions provided before the first item. Complete each item individually by first circling a number that best corresponds to your perception of where you fall along the continuum from 1 to 5 (s = self). Then circle the number that you think best represents the majority American value (o = other). Of course, there is no correct answer. After you have responded to each of the 20 items, compare your responses with a colleague, or with the whole staff. Do you see a pattern between your personal values and those you attribute to Americans in general? Are you able to reach a comfortable consensus with your colleagues? Are there items where consensus is impossible? Why? How does your attitude affect how you approach your students?

Activity 5.1
Cross-Cultural Analysis

Following each item you will find two rows of numbers. In the first row, circle the number that indicates the strength of your own position regarding this item (s = self). In the second row, circle the number that you think indicates the strength of the position of the general American public regarding this item (o = others).

1.	**Attitude toward people:**				
	Individual is most important				*Group is most important*
s	1	2	3	4	5
o	1	2	3	4	5
2.	**Attitude toward technology:**				
	Highly valued				*People more important*
s	1	2	3	4	5
o	1	2	3	4	5
3.	**Attitude toward time:**				
	Instant success and satisfaction is most important				*Persistence is most important*
s	1	2	3	4	5
o	1	2	3	4	5
4.	**Attitude toward achievement:**				
	Goal and accomplishment-oriented				*Human relations-oriented*
s	1	2	3	4	5
o	1	2	3	4	5
5.	**Attitude toward work:**				
	Work to live				*Live to work*
s	1	2	3	4	5
o	1	2	3	4	5

6.	**Attitude toward small group or family:**				
	Loyalty to family is most important				*Other relationships more important*
s	1	2	3	4	5
o	1	2	3	4	5

7.	**Style of communication:**				
	Polite, vague, indirect				*Frank, open, direct*
s	1	2	3	4	5
o	1	2	3	4	5

8.	**Attitude toward strangers:**				
	Complete distrust				*Great hospitality*
s	1	2	3	4	5
o	1	2	3	4	5

9.	**Attitude toward value of experience:**				
	Learn from mistakes				*Avoid mistakes at all costs*
s	1	2	3	4	5
o	1	2	3	4	5

10.	**Attitude toward change:**				
	Change is inevitable				*Impossible to achieve*
s	1	2	3	4	5
o	1	2	3	4	5

11.	**Attitude toward problem-solving:**				
	Rational, logical				*Instinctive, impulsive*
s	1	2	3	4	5
o	1	2	3	4	5

12.	**Attitude toward status, rank, and education:**				
	Based on heredity and seniority				*Earned by ability and hard work*
s	1	2	3	4	5
o	1	2	3	4	5

13.	**Attitude toward control of environment:**				
	Total control is possible				*Fatalistic*
s	1	2	3	4	5
o	1	2	3	4	5
14.	**Attitude toward relationship to others:**				
	Individual needs are most important				*Group needs most important*
s	1	2	3	4	5
o	1	2	3	4	5
15.	**Attitude toward authority:**				
	Resentment, rebellion				*Valued, respected*
s	1	2	3	4	5
o	1	2	3	4	5
16.	**Attitude toward meeting commitments (appointments, schedules, etc.):**				
	Casual, little concern				*Great concern*
s	1	2	3	4	5
o	1	2	3	4	5
17.	**Concern for status:**				
	Complete indifference				*Great concern*
s	1	2	3	4	5
o	1	2	3	4	5
18.	**Attitude toward maintenance of classroom discipline:**				
	Very strict, reliance on punishment				*Very permissive, reliance on student responsibility*
s	1	2	3	4	5
o	1	2	3	4	5
19.	**Attitude toward personal responsibility:**				
	Takes initiative, self-directed				*Waits for direction*
s	1	2	3	4	5
o	1	2	3	4	5

20.	**Attitude toward bureaucracy and red tape:**				
	A necessary inconvenience				*Unnecessary and intolerable*
s	1	2	3	4	5
o	1	2	3	4	5

Comments:

TEACHING CULTURE IN THE ADULT ESL CLASSROOM

What characterizes the typical adult ESL classroom is its diversity. How does the teacher attempt to reach each student when the classroom may contain students from a dozen or more distinct cultures? My suggestion is to start first with yourself.

Autobiographical Essay

Whether the adult educator has extensive cross-cultural experience, or little, a good first staff development activity to do even before entering the classroom for the first time is to write an autobiographical essay (Activity 5.2). The purpose of this assignment is to reflect on your personal history and those factors in your cultural environment that have helped to shape your values and attitudes today. This is not an easy assignment. In fact, a common complaint is that this assignment is difficult. Most adult ESL teachers have never had to reflect in this way. I offer to read the teachers' first draft and share my comments with them. I emphasize that this essay is not to be just a simple chronology of events.

Teachers should be reassured that what they write in their essay will remain confidential and will be shared with no one. This is important because often they will write about events that are embarrassing, painful, or otherwise too personal. Some of my graduate students have written about experiencing various forms of abuse as a child. Wives have written about controlling husbands. And parents have written about difficulties in raising children in today's society.

Most of us, however, only barely scratch the surface of reflecting on how the culture that surrounds us influences who we are as adult learners. The culture that surrounds us is like the air we breathe. We take it for granted until we are forced to leave it. So it is that adult ESL program directors will look to hire teachers who have had cross-cultural experiences, or can at least show evidence that they can successfully navigate this ocean of diversity. Having those experiences can make us more supportive of the adult English language learners who are often experiencing the difficulties of making a cross-cultural adjustment as they learn English.

Adult ESL teachers can use this same activity in their classrooms as a prompt for adult learners to talk about their own life experiences. Your adult students have a story to tell and they will tell it in a safe and secure environment.

Activity 5.2
Writing the Reflective Essay

Before we can more fully understand others as cultural beings, it is important to understand ourselves. What are our attitudes and beliefs about the world around us, and how did we come to hold these as our own? The purpose of this assignment is to explore ourselves as cultural beings. This is not a chronological report of the major events in your life. Rather, you should explore the major themes that mark your development, that have helped to determine who you are.

You may wish to organize this essay by viewing yourself as at the center of several concentric circles, each one representing a wider part of the world in which you live. This is just a suggestion.

- **Family**: How has your family influenced your development? What are some of the values and beliefs shared by members of your family that you hold onto? What about your religious beliefs?

- **Community**: Did you grow up in a small town or large city? In a rural, suburban, or urban setting? Do you attribute any of your attitudes, values, and beliefs to your community?
- **Nation**: Can you identify certain values and beliefs that you hold in common with the national or regional mainstream culture? Do you consider yourself a member of the dominant culture or a minority culture? How are your attitudes and beliefs different as a result of your membership in one or the other of these groups? Do you attribute any values and beliefs to your membership in a cohort with common experiences, such as baby boomers, generation X, the 60s, Post-9/11, or economic prosperity?
- **World**: Are there any universal characteristics or attributes of humans that you recognize as important to your own identity?
- **The role of culture in learning**. How has your culture influenced you as a learner? Do you learn in a specific way that is similar or different from the way that others learn? Conversely, are there teaching styles that you find more effective for you? Do you learn best in a student-centered or teacher-centered classroom? To what do you attribute this preference?

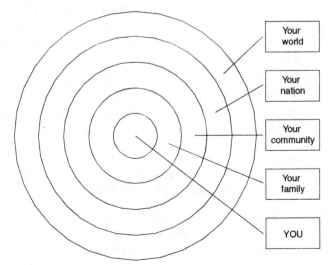

The Cultural Field Trip

Another activity that can be modified for use in the classroom, or as a staff development activity, is the cultural field trip (Activity 5.3). The cultural field trip can be conducted as a whole group activity at lower levels, or more advanced students can be encouraged to participate in pairs. What I describe here is the activity I assign my graduate students, but it would also be appropriate as a staff development activity. A major benefit would be to get novice and experienced teachers into the communities where their students live. Program administrators should feel free to adapt it to their own local community resources.

For the cultural field trip, participants are encouraged to find a partner. Together they decide on where to go for this field trip. Northern Illinois offers a wonderful assortment of cultures from the neighborhoods of Chicago to the many cities and towns in the rest of the region that have attracted growing communities of immigrants. All I require is that participants look for an item "of cultural significance" in the community they have selected. Find out from any of the locals all they can about that item. Bring that item back to the whole group where you will share your findings with your classmates or colleagues. However, the real task is to interact with members of the host community. What do you learn through this interaction that may give you valuable insights into the values and attitudes of the members of that host community? This assignment is consistently rated among the very favorite assignments for this course. This in spite of the fact that for many of these students the thought of entering some of these communities is a very intimidating proposition.

Activity 5.3
The Cultural Field Trip

The objective of this activity is to understand the behaviors, values, and ways of life of persons of another culture through learning about the cultural significance of items used by those persons. It could be adapted for use as a staff development activity or for use with advanced English language learners.

PARTICIPANTS
- Facilitator. All participants in teams of two or three.

MATERIALS
- None required.

SETTINGS
- A designated community that represents a culture which is unfamiliar to the team members.
- A meeting place for debriefing and discussion of results.

TIME
- A half-day for the field trip. Another several hours for the debriefing, depending on the number of teams and different communities visited.

PROCEDURE
- The facilitator will lead participants in a brainstorming session in which lists are developed which contain different items to be found within the unfamiliar community. These items might be certain kinds of medicine, items related to religion, recreation, food, household supplies and decoration, literature, cosmetics, music, commerce—each of which defines, in a small way, the people's behaviors, values, and ways of life.
- Participants should carry out their hunt in teams of two or three. They should learn as much as they can about how the item is used, so that they can demonstrate its use to others when they return to the next meeting.
- During the group debriefing, participants share the items and explain to each other what they have learned about their cultural importance. They also compare various experiences involved in carrying out the hunt—amusing incidents, cultural differences, hostile reactions, unexpected discoveries.
- If there are members of the learning group who came from the "target community," they can assist in explaining to the others about the culture of that community.

(Adapted from Henry Holmes and Stephen Guild (1971)).

Teaching for cross-cultural understanding in the classroom is never easy, especially with students with low-level oral and literacy skills. The following activities can be adapted for use at different levels. Some I have used with English language learners. They all incorporate communication skills in different ways.

Journal Writing

Journal writing has become a popular activity in the adult ESL classroom. It can be a vehicle for interpersonal communication between learner and teacher that provides authentic practice in written English. Unless the goal of the activity is to teach grammar, I would not recommend that you correct your students' writing in a journal activity. What you may find more effective is identifying problem areas in the students' writing and using these examples in other classroom activities that target language mechanics. Encourage your students to write whatever may be on their mind. But be prepared to write responses on a regular basis. The practice of responding to student writing in the journal is called the "dialogue journal" (Peyton & Reed, 1990) and is an effective technique for exploring social and cultural issues in the students' lives. Journal writing can be an effective tool for encouraging meaningful writing, especially at the intermediate level of the adult ESL curriculum.

Journal writing can also provide an excellent source of continuing personal staff development (Orem, 2001). By maintaining your own journal, you can enhance your observation skills as well as your ability to reflect on your teaching experience. A journal can provide a record of your experience which in turn helps you to build a database of personal reflection, thereby helping you to better understand outcomes in your everyday classroom practice.

Critical Incidents

Critical incidents are useful for generating discussion and critical thinking skills at all instructional levels (Brislin, Cushner, Cherrie, & Yong, 1986). Critical incidents can grow out of the students lived experiences and not necessarily out of a planned curriculum. Critical incidents are concisely stated scenarios that report an event or problem. There may, or may not, be one appropriate response or solution. The purpose of the critical incident is to engage the students in a discussion of the event or problem, preferably one experienced by a member of the class. The reported scenario should give just enough information to provide a starting point for discussion. Encourage the students to arrive at a consensus as to how to resolve this problem. Discuss strategies for how to avoid such problems in the future.

Activity 5.4 is a critical incident that could be adapted for a staff development exercise on cross-cultural communication. Or it could be used in an intermediate to advanced ESL class as a stimulus for discussion and cross-cultural analysis. The problem was provided by one of my students.

Activity 5.4
The Critical Incident

The Invitation to Dinner

Bob and Mary had just joined the staff of an international relief organization in the Philippines. After only several days, one of their Filipino co-workers invited them to his house for dinner and to meet his wife and parents. They were excited about this because they had dreamed of learning more about the host culture through these types of gatherings. As they were served the first course, Bob and Mary exchanged glances because, although they weren't sure of what they were being served, it did not appeal at all to their senses. Despite the insistence of their host, they avoided eating what was considered a true delicacy. Their co-worker's family was obviously disappointed by this refusal to share in this gesture of hospitality and generosity. In the weeks to follow, Bob and Mary noted an apparent coolness in their relationship with their host co-worker, but could not understand what they had done to offend him. Despite their attempts to find out directly from him if they had *offended him, he would always avoid any direct discussion of the topic, and never invited them back to his home.*

How would you have handled the situation if you were Bob or Mary? What typical American values (if any) are demonstrated by Bob and Mary? What typical Filipino values (if any) are exhibited by the hosts?

Open Discussions

Set aside some time in class at least once each week for an open discussion. Arrange chairs in a circle. The closer the chairs are, the better. Be sure you have presented ground rules for this activity so that everyone feels safe. You will also need to set rules to avoid one student dominating the discussion. Have a topic ready to go, but first allow students to suggest a topic. This should be a topic of some general interest. I would also suggest that the facilitator of any open-ended discussion be prepared to impose some ground rules for discussion. Here are some sample ground rules.

1. Respect everyone by maintaining confidentiality of what is said.

2. Refrain from the use of derogatory language.

3. Help ensure that all have an opportunity to participate in class discussions.

4. Let the teacher know your concerns and needs.

5. Help keep the class on focus.

6. Address your comments to the group, not the teacher.

7. Listen closely to others.

8. Maintain an open mind.

9. Use humor as long as it does not perpetuate cultural stereotypes.

10. Work hard at understanding the opinion of those with whom you disagree.

Values Clarification

Cross-cultural training began to flourish in the 1970s at the same time that the values-clarification movement was shaping educational curriculum at all levels. Therefore, it is not surprising that some effective values-clarification exercises have found their way into cross-cultural training programs. Activity 5.5 was originally developed by Professor Sidney Simon of the University of Massachusetts, and first appeared in a UNESCO training manual in 1971. It was later reprinted in a cross-cultural training manual, *Multicultural Education: A Cross-Cultural Training Approach* (Pusch, 1979).

Allow about 30 minutes for this staff development exercise. Simon's original objectives were to (1) help participants get acquainted with each other; (2) demonstrate through self-discovery how their decisions are determined by cultural values; (3) acquaint participants with specific cultural differences that exist among members of the group; and (4) stimulate awareness of problems in reaching consensus and listening to others.

Activity 5.5
The Parable

The leader will tell this parable involving five characters. The behavior of each character is intended to suggest a number of different values.

Rosemary is a girl of about 21 years of age. For several months she has been engaged to a young man named—let's call him Geoffrey. The problem she faces is that between her and her fiancé lies a river. No ordinary river mind you, but a deep, wide river infested with hungry crocodiles.

Rosemary ponders how she can cross the river. She thinks of a man she knows, who has a boat. We'll call him Sin-

bad. So she approaches Sinbad, asking him to take her across. He replies, "Yes, I'll take you across if you'll spend the night with me." Shocked at this offer, she turns to another acquaintance, a certain Frederick, and tells him her story. Frederick responds by saying, "Yes, Rosemary, I understand your problem—but— it's your problem, not mine."

Rosemary decides to return to Sinbad, and spend the night with him. In the morning, he takes her across the river.

Her reunion with Geoffrey is warm. But on the evening before they are to be married, Rosemary feels compelled to tell Geoffrey how she succeeded in getting across the river. Geoffrey responds by saying, "I wouldn't marry you if you were the last woman on earth."

Finally, at her wits' end, Rosemary turns to the last character, Dennis. Dennis listens to her story and says, "Well, Rosemary, I don't love you . . . but I will marry you." And that's all we know of the story.

After participants in this exercise have read the story, ask them to list the five characters in descending order from the person whose behavior is most approved to the person whose behavior is least approved. Divide the whole group into small groups of four or five and ask them to discuss the choices they made. As a group, try to reach a consensus as to the order of the characters, and identify a value that they would attach to the actions of each one. Ask one person from each group to restate the value suggested by the group member. Is the opinion accurately restated? Summarize the entire activity with these observations:

- Values come out of one's cultural background. They are often part of a person's unconscious behavior.
- Within any particular culture a person's values are usually very logical. They make sense in that culture.
- For these reasons we should be very cautious about making moral judgments about others' values.
- If we really want to understand someone else, we have to listen extremely well and try to get inside the other person. This is the reason for the question, "Is the opinion accurately

restated?" Those of you who would have to answer "not very" have some work to do.
• What are some other areas in life where people's values differ? (Pusch, 1979)

Simulation Exercises

There are many excellent published simulation exercises designed for examining cultural differences. Some are more easily facilitated in the ESL classroom. One of the better known exercises is *Bafá Bafá: A Cross-Cultural Simulation* (Bafá Bafá, n. d.). Participants replicate two cultures and struggle to accomplish goals that are incompatible with the other culture. One culture (Alpha) is based on characteristics that we might associate with a more traditional culture. The other culture (Beta) is based on characteristics of a "modern" or Western society. This simulation can be used effectively to demonstrate how cultural values have a profound effect on how people interact within a group, whether that be a classroom or an organization of any kind. To take full advantage of the power of this simulation, I would highly recommend that you allocate at least 90 minutes, and that you have a second facilitator to assist. It requires a minimum of 12 participants but works better if you have as many as 35 participants. I have facilitated this simulation in classes with 15 to 25 students, and at conferences with as many as 50 participants. You can find out more about *Bafá Bafá* online at www.simulationtrainingsystems.com. Or you can contact Simulation Training Systems at P.O. Box 910, Del Mar, CA 92014. Telephone 1-800-942-2900.

Another effective simulation activity is *Barnga: A Simulation Game on Culture Clashes* (Thiagarajan & Steinwachs, 1990). *Barnga* clarifies the need to understand cultural rules and how newcomers come to learn those rules. The activity consists of dividing the group into small groups of three or four members each. Give each group a deck of cards, aces through sevens. Give each group a sheet that gives the ground rules for the "tournament" they are about to begin. Last, give each group a set of rules for the card game they will be playing. What the participants don't know is that each group gets a slightly different set of rules. After practicing the card game, the rules are removed and participants are requested to refrain from use of oral language. After each round, players move according to the number of hands they have won at their table, thereby mixing the players and the rules they are playing by. After several rounds of the tournament, the facilitator calls a halt and gathers the players together for a debriefing.

I have used this activity with groups of adult educators and public school educators, from 15 to 150, as a way of demonstrating the notion of how we live according to a presumed set of rules. And when we enter new situations without a clear knowledge of the rules governing that situation, we can run into trouble by trying to apply old rules to these new situations. *Barnga* is available from Intercultural Press, P.O. Box 700 Yarmouth, Maine 04096-0700. Telephone 1-800-370-2665 or online at www.interculturalpress.com.

Videos

I have found certain videos to be effective staff development tools for teaching cross-cultural awareness. Each one of the following runs about one hour.

- *A Class Divided* (Peters, 1985). Originally broadcast in 1985, this PBS Frontline presentation focuses on the work of an elementary school teacher in rural Iowa, Jane Elliot, in confronting prejudice through the now famous brown-eyes, blue-eyes simulation exercise which she originally conducted with her third grade students in 1968. Beginning with a class reunion of some of the original participants, the video continues by showing how Elliot also applied her teaching principles to adults in a work setting. More information about *A Class Di-*

vided can be found online at www.pbs.org/wgbh/pages/frontline/shows/divided/.

- *American Tongues* (Alvarez & Kolker, 1987). This award-winning video is a humorous examination of language in the United States. Interviews with various linguists and regional writers, together with interviews with speakers of local dialects, make for an informative look at how culture influences the American language across the country. This video is available from the Center for New American Media, 22-D Hollywood Ave., Hohokus, NJ 07423. More information can be found online at www.cnam.com.

- *The Japanese Version* (Alvarez & Kolker, 1991). A surprising look at how one Asian country has adapted Western cultural ideas and objects. If you thought you knew Japan, you might be surprised at what you see. This 56-minute video is also available from the Center for New American Media.

- *Blue Collar and Buddha* (Siegel & Johnston, 1988). This 57-minute video is a look at the Rockford, Illinois, community in the 1980s with a focus on its Lao refugee and working class populations. Rockford is seen as a city with a history of immigration. However, with the waves of immigrants from Southeast Asia occurring simultaneously with a period of economic instability in the community in the 1970s and 80s, social dynamics between the immigrant and host culture communities began to change dramatically. This video is available from the National Asian American Telecommunications Association (NAATA). More information is available online at www.naatanet.org.

- *Cold Water* (Ogami, 1987). International students discuss the common problems they face at an American university. The phenomenon of culture shock is explained as a predictable phase of acculturation and strategies are suggested for easing the transition through this difficult experience. This 48-minute video can be ordered from Intercultural Press. Visit online at www.interculturalpress.com.

- *The Color of Fear* (Mun Wah, 1995). Eight men gather for a retreat at which they discuss their own struggles with racism.

This video sends a powerful message about the effects of racism as felt by a number of ethnic groups in America. This 90-minute video is available from Stir Fry Seminars and Consulting, 154 Santa Clara Ave., Oakland, CA 94610. Telephone 1-510-420-0292. Or visit them online at www.stirfryseminars.com.

The study of culture and how culture influences our values and behaviors is a fascinating activity. Careful reflection of your own culture can reveal a good deal of why you learn and teach the way you do. Adult educators who teach English language learners are constantly exposed to sharp differences in culture illustrated by differences in language. As adult learners acquire competency in the English language, they also begin to understand the values and actions of those who speak it as a first language. This is all the more reason why we as adult educators should attempt to learn another language, if only to become more aware of different world views, especially the world views of the students who see us as the gatekeepers to a better understanding of this new language and all it conveys.

SUMMARY

Culture plays a key role in how we communicate and how we learn. This chapter discusses Hofstede's dimensions of culture and how this framework may help explain behavior and attitudinal differences among students new to American classrooms. It then offers a number of activities-some for the classroom, others only for a program of staff development activities-that can help teachers and administrators alike to better understand how their own values and attitudes play out in the instruction of those who have different cultural systems. I close this chapter with names of specific activities, including a number of videos, which I have found helpful in clarifying values in cross-cultural contexts.

CHAPTER 6

Looking Forward

When I entered the field of adult ESL as a Peace Corps Volunteer over 30 years ago, there was no "profession" of teaching English as a second or foreign language. One could argue that there still is no profession of teaching English as a second or foreign language if we stick closely to the standard definitions of profession. What the field of practice has represented over these past 30 years is more a vocation than a profession. However, we have been steadily moving in the direction of professionalizing the field. We have developed a professional identity through our professional organizations. A knowledge base now exists through an expanding research agenda primarily conducted in conjunction with a growing number of teacher education programs in colleges and universities. The condition most in need of change is the common working condition for the overwhelming majority of adult ESL practitioners, characterized largely by its part-time nature.

The research base that has become the foundation of our practice has grown substantially over the last 30 years. The professional organization of TESOL, founded in 1966, is truly a worldwide professional association that provides an important voice for professional development and advocacy throughout the world on the behalf of second language teachers. The standards movement is pushing the field to adopt standards of practice for both teaching and teacher preparation that will strengthen our position vis-à-vis accrediting bodies and funding agencies. New technologies are enabling teacher educators, second language teachers, and materials developers to create inno-

vative approaches to teaching English language learners at all levels.

Yet, with all of these examples of progress toward a professional identity for the field as a whole, adult ESL teachers still lack professional recognition of their field in the form of full-time employment opportunities in those settings where most adult ESL instruction occurs. This, in turn, will continue to present an important barrier to developing a cadre of well-trained and effective teachers for programs in the United States.

DEVELOPING A RESEARCH BASE

A group of educators interested in research, teaching, and policy in adult ESL gathered in Washington, D.C., in December 1996 to draft a research agenda for the field (National Clearinghouse for ESL Literacy Education, 1998). Following extensive feedback sessions, a research agenda for adult ESL was developed for the express purposes of

1. Encouraging funding of specific research by public and private sources.

2. Providing guidance to researchers and encouraging collaboration for specific projects.

3. Focusing discussion of various priorities for the field of practice.

This research agenda provides clusters of questions divided into five major categories: adults as learners; program design and instruction; teacher preparation and staff development; learner assessment; and policy.

Adults as Learners

It is appropriate that this topic appear first in this agenda. Understanding adult learning is essential before planning instruction, preparing teachers, assessing learners, and establishing policy for the field. There have been many attempts to describe adult learners (Cross, 1981; Houle, 1972; Knowles, 1980). Much of this earlier literature sought to provide a basis on which to design instruction. This earlier research literature stopped short of looking at linguistic and cultural differences, but it did provide some useful data that gave insights into the barriers that all adult learners face, regardless of cultural and linguistic background.

Second language researchers (Ellis, 1985; Krashen, 1982; Larsen-Freeman & Long, 1991) have provided us with a variety of models of second language learning that might be applied to adults. But too often these models prove to be overly simplistic and fail to take into account the complexities facing adults in their life roles. Many of these models may be helpful in explaining how adults learn to speak, but they don't provide a useful model for literacy acquisition. Moreover, these models too often focus on the individual learner without regard for that person's specific social context. Model development has often been based on observations of English language learners who are already highly educated in a first language. These populations don't sufficiently represent the type of adult English language learner that is the greatest challenge to adult educators. These are the illiterate or semiliterate adults who have the least amount, if any, of successful formal schooling in their home language, and who are facing the greatest challenges in the workplace, often working multiple low-skilled jobs at less than minimum wage, without benefits.

Program Design and Instruction

We do know from our experience and available research that adult learners will be motivated to attend programs that are relevant to their most pressing needs:

- To find or hold jobs that can provide some hope for economic survival.
- To better understand the community services available to

them, including healthcare, police and fire protection, and education.

• To help their children in their own educational endeavors.

Instructional approaches used in current program designs available to adult learners often incorporate many of these aspects into the language taught in those programs. Terms used to describe such approaches include competency-based, task-based, and content-based (Crandall & Peyton, 1993; Richards & Rodgers, 2001).

Funding agencies should be interested in knowing how successful programs are in recruiting and retaining students, and in providing effective instruction that will result in students achieving their own goals as well as program goals more efficiently. This means that programs need to collect relevant data that will inform critical decision making. Unfortunately, effective program instruction (and data collection) is hampered by a lack of prepared instructors, or by trained instructors who exit programs all too frequently due to lack of satisfactory work conditions. Technology provides alternatives that didn't exist even a few years ago. I am thinking of some of the interactive computer-based programs that provide excellent supplementary work for learners. Some efforts have also been made to provide distance learning programs to adult learners. These efforts, in my opinion, though innovative and professional in their design, are unlikely to reach the population of adult learners that lack the strategies necessary for being self-directed learners. The difficult-to-reach learners need face-to-face instruction conducted by skilled teachers with well-designed materials.

Teacher Preparation and Staff Development

This area of the research agenda is directly related to the very nature of the field of practice, that the overwhelming majority of instructional jobs are part-time and do not offer teachers much hope for professional recognition or advancement. The combination of part-time work, difficult-to-reach students, limited or unavailable staff development, and sometimes dangerous or inadequate working conditions leads to high turnover among both teachers and administrators.

Some states have made excellent use of staff development funds to deal somewhat effectively with these conditions. Illinois has a system of service centers that provides ongoing staff development to local adult education programs throughout the state. In some instances this staff development is coupled with graduate-level university credit that will motivate some teachers to enroll in master's level programs in linguistics, literacy, or adult education. This is only one example. Nationwide, programs for professional development of adult educators vary in format, state funding, and assessment. Some states require certification, others have identified core competencies, while a few states provide no support for professional development activities (Tolbert, 2001).

Interest in adult education teacher preparation and staff development parallels current research in K-12 teacher education. Findings from these research efforts in the K-12 sector support the concept of ongoing professional development and emphasis on reflective practice. Ongoing professional development should include study of the English language, theories of second language acquisition (both oral language and literacy acquisition), adult learners and the social context in which they live and work, and teaching methodology and materials development that reflect the realities of the students' lives.

Given the inadequacy of staff development funding in many programs, I would suggest several staff development models that don't require a lot of money. Peer coaching is a model that has experienced some success in the K-12 sector. It requires administrative support and encouragement in the adult education sector to encourage instructors to commit to spending some time in observing each other's classrooms. Time commitment would include a pre-observation meeting to discuss specific behaviors to observe, an observation period that might last several hours or an entire class period, and a post-observation meeting to review what was observed. Peer coaching can be effective in that it is done for the purpose of providing peer support and feedback, without the fear of evaluation.

Another model of staff development that doesn't require

money is mentoring. In this model, a more experienced teacher is paired with a less experienced teacher. Time is spent observing each other during class time, and consulting each other outside of class time. Specific goals for mentoring should be well articulated and feedback given in a nonjudgmental way.

The third staff development model suggested by the research agenda is the reflective teaching model. This model combines research, staff development, and teaching in a simultaneous process. Program leaders can encourage reading the professional literature, attending professional conferences, designing classroom-based research efforts, and reflecting on those efforts to decide how to change practice based on available literature, observations, and data collection.

Research efforts in this area of teacher preparation could hold tremendous implications for current staff development programs. So much of what we do is based on past practice. It is time to rethink our models of professional development, given the unique circumstances under which so many adult educators labor.

Learner Assessment

Assessment and accountability, often used interchangeably in contemporary discussions of educational practice, are two of the most commonly uttered words by policy makers and funding agencies.

> States must establish more effective programs that prioritize accountability for results by setting challenging expectations for students, using meaningful assessments, and aligning instruction to meet those expectations. Clear standards in core academics of reading, mathematics, language arts and English language acquisition; aligned student assessments; and appropriate performance measures will drive program improvement that benefits students. New local accountability systems will ensure that the most qualified and effective providers receive Federal funds. (U.S. Department of Education, 2003, p. 2)

It is important that adult educators take heed. What is interpreted by many funding agencies as a lack of accountability on the part of programs to educate learners is often tied to results of assessment programs. The federal government's emphasis on assessment will lead states to create new assessment instruments and the identification of learner outcomes based on external criteria. The inevitable result will be a standardization of instruction across states and across the country.

The emphasis placed by funding agencies, such as the Department of Education, on quantitative data generated by assessment instruments needs to be tempered by inclusion of qualitative data at the local level generated by teacher observations, learner portfolios, and performance-based assessments. Such tools can be effective, but they are also time-consuming. Programs would need to depend on underpaid teachers, or overworked administrators, to collect, organize, and interpret such data. Standardized tools are all too seductive in providing data that can be used, appropriately or inappropriately, to judge progress of individuals in comparison to large groups of learners. Ironically, such well-known standardized measures as the SAT, TOEFL, and GRE are coming under increasing criticism by states and universities for not providing true indication of students' achievement or potential for success at the next level. Given the highly culturally based context of adult ESL, why should we think that similar standardized instruments will work any better for this population? Again, a major part of this problem is that the field lacks a sufficient cadre of trained teachers and curriculum developers needed before accurate assessment tools can be effectively used and interpreted.

Certainly we will eventually need tools by which to measure effectiveness of our work. But we shouldn't sacrifice the needs of the learners for the desired efficiency of assessment.

Policy

Policy initiatives at the state and national levels often complicate the work of adult ESL educators. It is no secret that a significant number of students enrolled in adult ESL programs have entered the United States without proper documentation. Since September 11, 2001, the federal government has tried to institute procedures to track noncitizens, making it more difficult for many adult learners already in this country to attend classes. Policy issues that constantly surface to affect the lives of adult ESL learners include immigration reform and citizenship, welfare reform and healthcare, and English as an official language and bilingual education. Other policy discussions influenced by adult ESL learners include employment and access to public education.

Of all the marginalized groups in the United States, the majority of adult ESL learners are among the most marginalized, largely because they do not vote and, therefore, have no voice at the policy table. Their presence in our communities presents us with difficult decisions regarding fair housing, education, healthcare, and access to other social services that most of us take for granted. They have to constantly fight prevailing perceptions that they do not speak English because they do not want to, and that they are "freeloading" off the welfare system because they don't pay taxes. If many of them do not speak English, it may be because they are working several jobs and are just too tired to undertake such a difficult language. And even if they are working at below minimum wage in a "cash economy" for an employer that does not deduct income or payroll taxes, they are still paying sales taxes when they buy food, clothes, gasoline, and all of the other goods and services required to live in the community.

One policy initiative that encapsulates many of these issues affecting English language learners is the attempt to make English the official language of the United States. Most people are surprised to learn that English is not the "official" language of the United States. The framers of our Constitution purposefully omitted any reference to an official language. Crawford (2004) provides an explanation by suggesting that "the framers of the Constitution believed that a democracy should leave language choices up to the people" (p. 83).

Throughout U.S. history, attempts to establish an official language usually come at times of high immigration and are linked to efforts to "Americanize" new immigrants. These periods in our history are commonly associated with high levels of prejudice against ethnic groups. Until 1914 German was commonly taught in many schools in the Midwest. In fact, Chicago offered German-English bilingual instruction until the start of World War I. But the war created ill will toward Germany, and German language instruction in this country was restricted as a result. Unfortunately, there are many examples of policy decisions in this country that are directed toward various ethnic and language groups, resulting in loss of language diversity. Ironically, there is no evidence that language diversity has threatened the unity of the country. In fact, lack of language diversity is often a criticism of Americans and is associated with an insular attitude toward the larger world.

Most recently, a number of states have linked bilingual education to threats to unity and the poor performance of certain language groups in schools. Proponents of bilingual education have tried to argue that forcing students to learn English through immersion, thereby failing to maintain their home language, has led to a generation of students who are unable to perform well in both English and their home language. This has created a new generation of adult learners in need of English language literacy instruction.

THE STANDARDS MOVEMENT ARRIVES

The standards movement in American education that started in the 1990s is often viewed as a mixed blessing. In this section I will discuss two initiatives that are part of the standards movement that could have a significant impact on adult English language learning programs in the next decade.

TESOL Standards

In spite of some of the problems associated with this movement, I believe the standards for adult education ESL programs adopted by TESOL (2003) can help to open the door toward

more professional recognition. Standard 7 attempts to hold employers accountable for hiring qualified staff and for providing
them with appropriate employment conditions.

7. Standards for Employment Conditions and Staffing

A. *The program supports compensation and benefits commen-*
   surate with those of instructional and other professional
   staff with comparable positions and qualifications within
   similar institutions.

   In Illinois the major provider for adult ESL is the
   community college system. Unfortunately, community colleges are increasing the proportion of their instructional
   staff that is part-time. Therefore, this standard by itself is
   not going to ensure that adult ESL teachers are adequately
   compensated. But it is an important statement to providers
   that ESL programs are not to be treated differently than
   traditional core programs carrying credit toward degrees.

B. *The program has in place policies and procedures that en-*
   sure professional treatment of staff.

   This standard speaks to the need for programs to have
   in place programs of staff evaluation. Good staff evaluation procedures, if done properly, can also be useful as a
   staff development tool. Progressive employers recognize
   the need to provide staff development even to part-time
   teachers. This can include subsidizing their travel to and
   participation in professional conferences. It can also include providing local staff development activities for which
   staff are fairly compensated. It should also include fair
   procedures for hiring and firing staff. (See also *8: Stan-*
   dards for Professional Development and Staff Evaluation,
   pp. 23–24.)

C. *The program supports a safe and clean working environ-*
   ment.

   Normally one wouldn't think of a teaching environment as unsafe or unclean. However, many adult ESL
   teachers have found themselves in isolated satellite centers
   working in unsafe neighborhoods where even their own

students might be afraid to go out at night. It is not un-heard of for an adult ESL teacher working onsite in a work-place program to have experienced an unsafe or unclean environment. This standard attempts to ensure a basic level of security and safety that is necessary for learning.

The next subset of three standards speaks to the topic of staffing.

D. *The program recruits and hires qualified instructional staff with training in the theory and methodology of teaching ESL. Qualifications may vary according to local agency re-quirements and type of instructional position (e.g., paid teacher, volunteer).*

In practice there is wide variation for how providers interpret the meaning of qualified instructor. Some provid-ers may want someone with a master's degree in TESOL or applied linguistics, for example, to teach part-time. Some providers may be satisfied with someone who is simply willing to work with this population. If the provider al-ready has minimum qualifications (such as a B.A. degree), then the program will be required to find someone with a B.A. degree. But there is usually sufficient flexibility built into job descriptions that a qualified person may not be one with any training in the field. Most providers I know try to balance their definition of a qualified instructor with the reality that they may only be able to offer part-time em-ployment. Above all, the needs of the learners to receive quality instruction by well-prepared teachers must be given the greatest priority.

E. *The program recruits and hires qualified administrative, in-structional, and support staff who have appropriate train-ing in cross-cultural communication, reflect the cultural di-versity of the learners in the program, and have experience with or awareness of the specific needs of adult English learners in their communities*

If you look at the statistics of who works as adminis-trators, instructors, and support staff in adult ESL, you are likely to find one common theme. Instructors tend to be white, middle-class, and female. She may or may not speak another language fluently, but she is very unlikely to be someone who is herself a person who learned English as a second language. In larger suburban programs, an adult ESL instructor is unlikely to be familiar with the communities from which learners are recruited. Keep in mind that students tend to live in working class neighborhoods where rents are relatively lower, and where immigrants tend to cluster. Instructors tend to be middle-class and by definition live in middle-class neighborhoods. Likewise, many adult ESL teachers who attempt to make a living from patching together several part-time positions (the "Road Scholar") may travel as many as 60 miles or more to teach in one day. How can they be aware of the specific needs of their learners within the learners' communities?

F. *The program recruits and hires qualified support staff to ensure effective program operation.*

Support staff could include secretaries, counselors, workplace coordinators, volunteers and volunteer coordinators, or any one of a number of different positions that provide support to the basic mission of the program. Some adult ESL programs will work hard to hire support staff from among the graduates of their programs. This helps the program to reflect the cultural diversity of the community that they serve. It also helps the program to provide bilingual support for newly arrived immigrants.

Equipped for the Future

Equipped for the Future is an initiative of the National Institute for Literacy (NIFL) in response to Goal 6 of the National Educational Goals Panel. Goal 6 stated that by the year 2000 all adults would be literate. NIFL sent an open letter in January 1994 to teachers, tutors, and adult learners across the country asking them simply to answer the question: What is it that adults need to know and be able to do in order to be literate, compete in the global economy, and exercise the rights and responsibilities of citizenship? (Stein, 2000, p. 5). Within several months, more than 1500 adult students responded with their personal stories. From these responses, NIFL began the process of building a framework that would eventually result in a standards-based curriculum for adult learning called Equipped for the Future. With its four purposes for learning, and its 16 content standards, it is the most ambitious attempt to date at producing a national curriculum for adult learners.

ARE YOU READY FOR THE TECHNOLOGY?

The revolution in computer-based and Web-based technologies over the last 10 years has affected second language teaching and teacher education as well. Interactive materials allow learners to engage in more self-directed learning activities. One of my favorite examples of interactive computer-based technologies designed for adult English language learners is the English Language Learning and Instruction System™, simply known as ELLIS. This product consists of modules on CD-ROM that introduce and reinforce aspects of culture and language to the adult learner in an interactive format that can be easily mastered by most students in a short time. Students can practice pronunciation as they hear the sounds, record their own responses, and observe diagrams of the human mouth as it produces the sounds. Other modules reinforce grammar and vocabulary building through lessons that are adult-oriented. Different levels of this product are designed for instruction of younger school-age children and adults in business settings. For more information about this product, visit www.ellis.com.

The World Wide Web provides many excellent resources for teachers and students alike to supplement instruction of English language learners. Among the Web sites designed for adult English language learners, one of the most popular is Dave's Café (www.eslcafe.com). Created and operated by Dave Sperling, it includes chat rooms, job listings, classroom resources for teachers, FAQ (frequently asked questions) pages, and much more. Sperling has also written several useful guides for teachers and students, including *The Internet Guide for English Language Teachers* (1997), and *Dave Sperling's Internet Guide* (1998).

For me the past 30 years have seen the field move from "high tech" defined as flannel boards in my Peace Corps classroom, to ELLIS™, a computer-based software program, or *Crossroads Café*, an interactive video program designed for adult English language learners and broadcast over public television. These programs are expensive and often require collaboration between government agencies and private commercial vendors to produce the quality of product that meets the needs of programs, employers, and the adult learner.

As programs struggle to find qualified adult educators to teach English, administrators may exert greater pressure on graduate programs or staff development agencies to develop online modules for teacher training. Some programs can't predict when they will need to hire ESL instructors. Refugees may be displaced overnight. Some of them end up in a community due to the hospitality of a local church or community agency. Unfortunately, the track record for student retention in online instruction is not great. And there is no evidence that new teachers who have received training online are as effective as those who have experienced staff development in traditional face-to-face formats. But with increasing pressures on local programs to provide English language instruction, and with more sophisticated online technologies, we will see an increasing reliance on web-based training programs in the future (DuCharme-Hansen & Dupin-Bryant, 2004).

THE FORCE OF LEGISLATION

Perhaps the most telling evidence of how the field of adult ESL will take shape in the near future is in the language of the reauthorization bill for the Adult Education and Family Literacy Act entitled *A Blueprint for Preparing America's Future: The Adult Basic and Literacy Education Act of 2003* (U.S. Department of Education, 2003). Anyone familiar with the language of the reauthorization of the Elementary and Secondary

Education Act of 2001 (PL 107–110), known as No Child Left Behind (NCLB) , will not be surprised by the language of the proposed Adult Basic and Literacy Education Act (ABLE).

Key terms and phrases of the proposed legislation held in common with NCLB include "high-quality," "funding what works," "research-based programs," and "reduce bureaucracy." However, a careful reading of the language will reveal some significant differences. NCLB uses "high-quality" to describe not only the quality of programs, but also the quality of instruction. To that end, NCLB places strict goals on the preparation of classroom teachers equating high-quality to certification of teachers in subject matter. The reauthorization language of ABLE is comparatively silent on teacher quality, but stresses program quality throughout. In fact, there is only one brief reference to teacher quality in ABLE (U.S. Department of Education, 2003).

> State plans will require States to provide a description of their standards for instructional staff qualifications and how the eligible agency will provide and continuously improve instructional staff qualifications through professional development and training on scientifically based instructional practices. (p. 9)

"Funding what works," and "scientifically based research" are often found together in this reauthorized legislation. Evidence of what works will need to be grounded in research that meets an acceptable standard for quality in the Department of Education.

> ... funds reserved for national activities will support rigorous research that uses accepted practices of scientific inquiry to investigate the validity of theories and the effectiveness of practices in adult basic and literacy education. This research creates scientifically valid research findings that can provide the basis for improving instruction and learning. (p. 11)

Anecdotal evidence or purely descriptive research is no longer sufficient. There will be a new emphasis on results of highly controlled experimental designs demonstrating cause and effect. This "gold standard" for research has already generated concern among second language researchers and teacher educators, who tend to rely on qualitative methods in their own research. After all, what should be driving the research in the field is not the research method and the ideology of the funding agency, but the questions we ask and the problems we need to investigate to help teachers be more effective in their classrooms.

There will be new standards for both program and student accountability. Programs that do not meet goals established by the state will risk losing federal funding.

> States will establish more effective systems that make accountability for results a priority by setting challenging expectations for students, using meaningful assessments, and aligning instruction to meet those expectations. Clear standards in core academics of reading, mathematics, language arts and English language acquisition; aligned student assessments; and appropriate performance measures will drive program improvement that benefits students. New local accountability systems will ensure that only the most qualified providers receive Federal funds. (p. 4)

In moving toward greater accountability, states will establish standards that all programs will adhere to. Some will say this is good for a mobile student population. It also makes sense in terms of interpreting assessment results. It will allow states to compare program outcomes from urban centers as well as rural districts. Unfortunately, this is bound to create new problems for local programs, similar to what has happened under NCLB. There is a strong tradition of local control of curriculum in the United States. This is true for both K-12 programs as well as adult education programs. Under this legislation, we are going to see movement toward statewide curricula driven by federal mandate. Could a nationwide curriculum for adult ESL be far behind?

SUMMARY

In this chapter I examine elements of our work that have contributed to our professional identity and that will continue to influence our work as language teaching professionals for the next decade or more. *Research Agenda for Adult ESL* (National Clearinghouse, 1998) has identified the importance of focused study of adults as learners, program design and instruction, teacher preparation and staff development, learner assessment, and policy. Each of these areas contains a rich source of questions for continuing study that will help teachers and administrators better understand the nature of our work with adult English language learners.

I discuss how the standards recently published by TESOL can provide guidance for program administrators as they advocate for teachers and learners. Another example of a standards-based initiative with ties to the competency-based Adult Performance Level Study of the 1970s is *Equipped for the Future*, developed by the National Institute for Literacy.

Technology is playing an increasing role in helping teachers become more effective instructors. I offered several current examples of technology and Web sites that can support your teaching. Finally, I encouraged teachers and administrators to be knowledgeable of the changing language of the laws that govern and fund our activities. The world of teaching English language learners is changing rapidly. What worked in 1975 may not work in 2005. Teachers and administrators need to continuously take advantage of the resources available through professional organizations, staff development agencies, and the World Wide Web. At times we can feel overwhelmed by this deluge of sometimes conflicting data. Always keep in mind that your ultimate goal is the success of those adult English language learners that you are teaching. Good luck!

APPENDIX A

National Reporting System
ESL Functional Levels

The National Reporting System (NRS, 2001) uses the following assessment programs as benchmarks for comparing data:

- CASAS: the Comprehensive Adult Student Assessment System. The CASAS skill level descriptors show a continuum of skills from beginning through advanced adult secondary. They provide descriptions of adults' general job-related ability in reading, mathematics, oral communication, and writing. The Skill Level Descriptors explain in general terms what most learners can accomplish at the CASAS scale score level in a specific skill area. (www.casas.org)
- SPL: Student Performance Levels. (See Appendix B for an explanation)
- BEST: Basic English Skills Test. This is designed for adult ESL learners at the survival and pre-employment skills level; different versions assess oral communication (Oral BEST) and literacy (Literacy BEST). (www.cal.org/BEST/)
- BEST Plus: A computer-based version of the BEST. (www.cal.org/bestplus/)

Speaking and Listening	Basic Reading and Writing	Functional and Workplace Skills	Benchmarks
Beginning ESL Literacy Individual cannot speak or understand English, or understands only isolated words or phrases.	Individual has no or minimal reading or writing skills in any language. May have little or no comprehension of how print corresponds to spoken language and may have difficulty using a writing instrument.	Individual functions minimally or not at all in English and can communicate only through gestures or a few isolated words, such as name and other personal information; may recognize only common signs or symbols (e.g., stop sign, product logos); can handle only very routine entry-level jobs that do not require oral or written communication in English. There is no knowledge or use of computers or technology.	CASAS (Life Skills): 180 and below SPL (Speaking): 0–1 SPL (Reading and Writing): 0–1 Oral BEST: 0–15 Literacy BEST: 0–7 BEST Plus: below 401

Speaking and Listening	Basic Reading and Writing	Functional and Workplace Skills	Benchmarks
Beginning ESL Individual can understand frequently used words in context and very simple phrases spoken slowly and with some repetition; there is little communicative output and only in the most routine situations; little or no control over basic grammar; survival needs can be communicated simply, and there is some understanding of simple questions.	Individual can recognize, read and write numbers and letters, but has a limited understanding of connected prose and may need frequent re-reading; can write a limited number of basic sight words and familiar words and phrases; may also be able to write simple sentences or phrases, including very simple messages. Can write basic personal information. Narrative writing is disorganized and unclear; inconsistently uses simple punctuation (e.g., periods, commas, question marks); contains frequent errors in spelling.	Individual functions with difficulty in situations related to immediate needs and in limited social situations; has some simple oral communication abilities using simple learned and repeated phrases; may need frequent repetition; can provide personal information on simple forms; can recognize common forms of print found in the home and environment, such as labels and product names; can handle routine entry level jobs that require only the most basic written or oral English communication and in which job tasks can be demonstrated. There is minimal knowledge or experience using computers or technology.	CASAS (Life Skills): 181–200 SPL (Speaking): 2–3 SPL (Reading and Writing): 2–4 Oral BEST: 16–41 Literacy BEST: 8–46 BEST Plus: 401–438

Speaking and Listening	Basic Reading and Writing	Functional and Workplace Skills	Benchmarks
Low Intermediate ESL Individual can understand simple learned phrases and limited new phrases containing familiar vocabulary spoken slowly with frequent repetition; can ask and respond to questions using such phrases; can express basic survival needs and participate in some routine social conversations, although with some difficulty; has some control of basic grammar.	Individual can read simple material on familiar subjects and comprehend simple and compound sentences in single or linked paragraphs containing a familiar vocabulary; can write simple notes and messages on familiar situations, but lacks clarity and focus. Sentence structure lacks variety, but shows some control of basic grammar (e.g., present and past tense), and consistent use of punctuation (e.g., periods, capitalization).	Individual can interpret simple directions and schedules, signs, and maps; can fill out simple forms, but needs support on some documents that are not simplified; can handle routine entry level jobs that involve some written or oral English communication, but in which job tasks can be demonstrated. Individual can use simple computer programs and can perform a sequence of routine tasks given directions using technology (e.g., fax machine, computer).	CASAS (Life Skills): 201–210 SPL (Speaking): 4 SPL (Reading and Writing): 5 Oral BEST: 42–50 Literacy BEST: 47–53 BEST Plus: 439–472

Speaking and Listening	Basic Reading and Writing	Functional and Workplace Skills	Benchmarks
High Intermediate ESL Individual can understand learned phrases and short new phrases containing familiar vocabulary spoken slowly and with some repetition; can communicate basic survival needs with some help; can participate in conversation in limited social situations and use new phrases with hesitation; relies on description and concrete terms. There is inconsistent control of more complex grammar.	Individual can read text on familiar subjects that have a simple and clear underlying structure (e.g., clear main idea, chronological order); can use context to determine meaning; can interpret actions required in specific written directions, can write simple paragraphs with main idea and supporting detail on familiar topics (e.g., daily activities, personal issues) by recombining learned vocabulary and structures; can self and peer edit for spelling and punctuation errors.	Individual can meet basic survival and social needs, can follow simple oral and written instruction and has some ability to communicate on the telephone on familiar subjects; can write messages and notes related to basic needs; complete basic medical forms and job applications; can handle basic jobs that involve basic oral instruction in tasks that can be clarified orally. The individual can work with or learn basic computer software, such as word processing; can follow simple instructions for using technology.	CASAS (Life Skills): 211–220 SPL (Speaking): 5 SPL (Reading and Writing): 6 Oral BEST: 51–57 Literacy BEST: 54–65 BEST Plus: 473–506

Speaking and Listening	Basic Reading and Writing	Functional and Workplace Skills	Benchmarks
Low Advanced ESL			
Individual can converse on many everyday subjects and some subjects with unfamiliar vocabulary, but may need repetition, rewording, or slower speech; can speak creatively, but with hesitation; can clarify general meaning by rewording and has control of basic grammar; understands descriptive and spoken narrative and can comprehend abstract concepts in familiar contexts.	Individual is able to read simple descriptions and narratives on familiar subjects or from which new vocabulary can be determined by context; can make some minimal inferences about familiar texts and compare and contrast information from such texts, but not consistently. The individual can write simple narrative descriptions and short essays on familiar topics, such as customs in native country; has consistent use of basic punctuation, but makes grammatical errors with complex structures.	Individual can function independently to meet most survival needs and can communicate on the telephone on familiar topics; can interpret simple charts and graphics; can handle jobs that require simple oral and written instructions, multi-step diagrams, and limited public interaction. The individual can use all basic software applications, understand the impact of technology, and select the correct technology in a new situation.	CASAS (Life Skills): 221–235 SPL (Speaking): 6 SPL (Reading and Writing): 7 Oral BEST: 58–64 Literacy BEST: 65 and above BEST Plus: 507–540

Speaking and Listening	Basic Reading and Writing	Functional and Workplace Skills	Benchmarks
High Advanced ESL Individual can understand and participate effectively in face-to-face conversations on everyday subjects spoken at normal speed; can converse and understand independently in survival, work, and social situations; can expand on basic ideas in conversation, but with some hesitation; can clarify general meaning and control basic grammar, although still lacks total control over complex structures.	Individual can read authentic materials on everyday subjects and can handle most reading related to life roles; can consistently and fully interpret descriptive narratives on familiar topics and gain meaning from unfamiliar topics and uses increased control of language and meaning-making strategies to gain meaning of unfamiliar texts. The individual can write multi-paragraph essays with a clear introduction and development of ideas; writing contains well-formed sentences, appropriate mechanics and spelling and few grammatical errors.	Individual has a general ability to use English effectively to meet most routine social and work situations; can interpret routine charts, graphs, and tables and complete forms; has high ability to communicate on the telephone and understand radio and television; can meet work demands that require reading and writing and can interact with the public. The individual can use common software and learn new applications; can define the purpose of software and select new applications appropriately; can instruct others in use of software and technology.	CASAS (Life Skills): 236–245 SPL (Speaking): 7 SPL (Reading and Writing): 8 Oral BEST: 65 and above BEST Plus: above 540

APPENDIX B

Student Performance Level Descriptors

This appendix presents the student performance level (SPL) descriptors (Office of Refugee Resettlement, 1985).

Level	General Language Ability	Listening Comprehension	Oral Communication
0	No ability whatsoever	No ability whatsoever	No ability whatsoever
1	Functions minimally, if at all, in English. Can handle only very routine entry-level jobs that do not require oral communication, and in which all tasks can be easily demonstrated. A native speaker used to dealing with limited English speakers can rarely communicate with a person at this level.	Understands only a few isolated words, and extremely simple learned phrases.	Vocabulary limited to a few isolated words. No control of grammar.
2	Functions in a very limited way in situations related to immediate needs. Can handle only routine entry-level	Understands a limited number of very simple learned phrases, spoken slowly with frequent repetitions.	Expresses a limited number of immediate survival needs using very simple learned phrases.

Level	General Language Ability	Listening Comprehension	Oral Communication
	jobs that do not require oral communication, and in which all tasks can be easily demonstrated. A native English speaker used to dealing with limited English speakers will have great difficulty communicating with a person at this level.		
3	Functions with some difficulty in situations related to immediate needs. Can handle routine entry-level jobs that involve only the most basic oral communication, and in which all tasks can be demonstrated. A native English speaker used to dealing with limited English speakers will have great difficulty communicating with a person at this level.	Understands simple learned phrases, spoken slowly with frequent repetitions.	Expresses immediate survival needs using simple learned phrases.
4	Can satisfy basic survival needs and a few very routine social demands. Can handle entry-level jobs that involve some simple oral communica-	Understands simple learned phrases easily, and some simple new phrases containing familiar vocabulary, spoken slowly with frequent repetitions.	Expresses basic survival needs including asking and responding to related questions, using both learned and a limited number of new

Level	General Language Ability	Listening Comprehension	Oral Communication
	tion, but in which tasks can be easily demonstrated. A native English speaker used to dealing with limited English speakers will have difficulty communicating with a person at this level.		phrases. Participants in basic conversations in a few very routine social situations. Speaks with hesitation and frequent pauses. Some control of basic grammar.
5	Can satisfy basic survival needs and some limited social demands. Can handle jobs and job training that involve following simple oral instructions but in which most tasks can also be demonstrated. A native English speaker used to dealing with limited English speakers will have some difficulty communicating with a person at this level.	Understands learned phrases easily and short new phrases containing familiar vocabulary spoken slowly with repetition. Has limited ability to understand on the telephone.	Functions independently in most face-to-face basic survival situations but needs some help. Asks and responds to direct questions on familiar and some unfamiliar subjects. Still relies on learned phrases but also uses new phrases but with hesitation and pauses. Communicates on the phone to express a limited number of survival needs, but with some difficulty. Participates in basic conversations in a limited number of social situations. Can occasionally clarify general meaning by simple rewording. Increasing, but inconsistent control of basic grammar.

Level	General Language Ability	Listening Comprehension	Oral Communication
6	Can satisfy most survival needs and limited social demands. Can handle jobs and job training that invovle following simple oral and written instructions and diagrams. A native English speaker not used to dealing with limited English speakers will be able to communicate with a person at this level on familiar topics, but with some difficulty and some effort.	Understands conversations containing some unfamiliar vocabulary on many everyday subjects, with a need for repetition, rewording or slower speech. Has some ability to understand without face-to-face contact (such as on the telephone).	Functions independently in most survival situations, but needs some help. Relies less on learned phrases; speaks with creativity, but with hesitation. Communicates on the phone on familiar subjects but with some difficulty. Participates with some confidence in social situations when addressed directly. Can sometimes clarify general meaning by rewording. Control of basic grammar evident, but inconsistent; may attempt to use more difficult grammar but with almost no control.
7	Can satisfy survival needs and routine work and social demands. Can handle work that involves following oral and simple written instructions in familiar and some unfamiliar situations. A native English speaker not used to dealing with limited English speakers can generally	Understands conversations on most everyday subjects at normal speed when addressed directly; may need repetition, rewording, or slower speech. Understands routine work-related conversations. Increasing ability to understand without face-to-face contact	Functions independently in survival and many social and work situations, but may need help occasionally. Communicates on the phone on familiar subjects. Expands on basic ideas in conversation, but still speaks with hesitation while searching for appropriate vocabu-

Level	General Language Ability	Listening Comprehension	Oral Communication
	communicate with a person at this level on familiar topics.	(telephone, TV, radio). Has difficulty following conversation between native speakers.	lary and grammar. Clarifies general meaning easily, and can sometimes convey exact meaning. Controls basic grammar, but not more difficult grammar.
8	Can participate effectively in social and familiar work situations. A native English speaker not used to dealing with limited English speakers can communicate with a person at this level on almost all topics.	Understands general conversation and conversation on technical subjects in own field. Understands without face-to-face contact (telephone, TV, radio); may have difficulty following rapid or colloquial speech. Understands most conversations between native speakers; may miss details if speech is very rapid or colloquial or if subject is unfamiliar.	Participates effectively in practical and social conversation and in technical discussions in own field. Speaks fluently in both familiar and unfamiliar situations; can handle problem situations. Conveys and explains exact meaning of complex ideas. Good control of grammar.
9	Can participate fluently and accurately in practical, social, and work situations. A native English speaker not used to dealing with limited English speakers can communicate easily with a person at this level.	Understands almost all speech in any context. Occasionally confused by highly colloquial or regional speech.	Approximates a native speaker's fluency and ability to convey own ideas precisely, even in unfamiliar situations. Speaks without effort. Excellent control of grammar with no apparent patterns of weakness.

Level	General Language Ability	Listening Comprehension	Oral Communication
10	Ability equal to that of a native speaker of the same socio-economic level.	Equal to that of a native speaker of the same socio-economic level.	Equal to that of a native speaker of the same socio-economic level.

REFERENCES

Alvarez, L., & Kolker, A. (Producer/Director). (1987). *American tongues* [Video]. (Available from The Center for New American Media, 22-D Hollywood Ave., Hohokus, NJ 07423)

Alvarez, L., & Kolker, A. (Producer/Director). (1991). *The Japanese Version* [Video]. (Available from The Center for New American Media, 22-D Hollywood Ave., Hohokus, NJ 07423)

Asher, J. (1977). *Learning another language through actions: The complete teacher's guidebook.* Los Gatos, CA: Sky Oaks Productions.

Auerbach, E. R. (1992). *Making meaning, making change: Participatory curriculum development for adult ESL literacy.* McHenry, IL and Washington, DC: Delta Systems and Center for Applied Linguistics.

Auerbach, E. R. (1996). *Adult ESL/literacy from the community to the community: A guidebook for participatory literacy training.* Mahwah, NJ: Lawrence Erlbaum Associates.

Bafá Bafá. (n. d.). Available: www.simulationtrainingsystems.com.

BASIC English Skills Test (BEST). (n. d.). Washington, D.C.: Center for Applied Linguistics. Available: www.cal.org/BEST/

Bodman, J. (1979). Student-centering education: The gentle revolution in ESL teaching. In D. E. Bartley (Ed.), *The adult basic education TESOL handbook.* New York: Collier Macmillan.

Bouchard, D., et al. (1974). *Reading English as a second language and the adult learner.* Fall River, MA: Bristol Community College. (ERIC Document Reproduction Service No. ED 098510)

Brinkley, E. H. (1998). What's religion got to do with attacks on whole language? In K. S. Goodman (Ed.), *In defense of good teaching: What teachers need to know about the "Reading Wars."* York, ME: Stenhouse Publishers.

Brislin, R. W., Cushner, K., Cherrie, C., & Yong, M. (1986). *Intercultural interactions: A practical guide.* Beverly Hills, CA: Sage Publications.

Brown, H. D. (2000). *Principles of language teaching and learning* (4th ed.). New York: Addison Wesley Longman.

Brown, H. D. (2004). *Language assessment: Principles and classroom practices*. New York: Longman.

Brown, J. D. (1995). *The elements of language curriculum: A systematic approach to program development*. Boston: Heinle and Heinle Publishers.

Brumfit, C., & Johnson, K. (Eds.) (1979). *The communicative approach to language teaching*. Oxford: Oxford University Press.

Burt, M., Peyton, J. K., & Adams, R. (2003). *Reading and adult English language learners: A review of the research*. Washington, DC: Center for Applied Linguistics.

Casanave, C. P. & Schecter, S. R. (Eds.) (1997). *On becoming a language educator: Personal essays on professional development*. Mahwah, NJ: Lawrence Erlbaum Associates.

Comprehensive Adult Student Assessment System (CASAS). (n. d.). Available: www.casas.org

Crandall, J., & Peyton, J. K. (Eds.). (1993). *Approaches to adult ESL literacy instruction*. McHenry, IL & Washington, DC: Center for Applied Linguistics and Delta Systems.

Crawford, J. (2004). *Educating English language learners: Language diversity in the classroom.* (5th ed.). Los Angeles, CA: Bilingual Education Services, Inc.

Cross, K. P. (1981). *Adults as learners: Increasing participation and facilitating learning*. San Francisco: Jossey-Bass.

Curran, C. A. (1976). *Counseling-learning in second languages*. Apple River, IL: Apple River Press.

Dave's Café [On-line]. Available: www.eslcafe.com

Dixon, C. N., & Nessel, D. (1983). *Language experience approach to reading (and writing): Language-experience reading for second language learners*. Hayward, CA: Alemany Press.

DuCharme-Hansen, B., & Dupin-Bryant, P. (2004). *Web-based distance education for adults*. Malabar, FL: Krieger Publishing Company.

Ellis, R. (1985). *Understanding second language acquisition*. Oxford: Oxford University Press.

English Language Learning System, Inc. (ELLIS). (n. d.). Available: www.ellis.com

Freeman, D., & Richards, J. C. (Eds.). (1996). *Teacher learning in language teaching*. Cambridge: Cambridge University Press.

Freire, P. (1970). *Pedagogy of the oppressed*. New York: Seabury Press.

Fries, C. C. (1945). *Teaching and learning English as a foreign language*. Ann Arbor: University of Michigan Press.

Fry, E. (1968). A readability formula that saves time. *Journal of Reading, 11* (April), 513–16, 575–77.

Gallo, M. L. (2004). *Reading the world of work: A learner-centered approach to workplace literacy*. Malabar, FL: Krieger Publishing Company.

Gattegno, C. (1972). *Teaching foreign languages in schools: The silent way* (2nd ed.). New York: Educational Solutions.

Gebhard, J. R., & Oprandy, R. (1999). *Language teaching awareness: A guide to exploring beliefs and practices*. Cambridge: Cambridge University Press.

Goodman, K. (1986). *What's whole in whole language?* Portsmouth, NH: Heinemann Educational Books.

Hofstede, G. (2001). *Culture's consequences: Comparing values, behaviors, institutions, and organizations across nations* (2nd ed.). Thousand Oaks, CA: Sage Publications.

Holmes, H., & Guild, S. (Eds.). (1971). *A manual of teaching techniques for intercultural education*. Paris: UNESCO.

Houle, C. O. (1972). *The design of education*. San Francisco: Jossey-Bass.

Hymes, D. (1971). Competence and performance in linguistic theory. In R. Huxley & E. Ingram (Eds.), *Language acquisition: Models and methods*. London: Academic Press.

Johnson, D. M., & Roen, D. H. (Eds.). (1989). *Richness in writing: Empowering ESL students*. New York: Longman.

Johnson, K. E., & Golombek, P. R. (Eds.). (2002). *Teachers' narrative inquiry as professional development*. Cambridge: Cambridge University Press.

Jordan, D. R. (1996). *Teaching adults with learning disabilities*. Malabar, FL: Krieger Publishing Company.

Kalmar, T. M. (2001). *Illegal alphabets and adult biliteracy: Latino migrants crossing the linguistic border*. Malwah, NJ: Lawrence Erlbaum Associates.

Kelley, C., & Meyers, J. (1993). *The cross-cultural adaptability inventory*. Chicago: Pearson Reid London House [On-line]. Available: www.pearsonreidlondonhouse.com/assessments/ccai.htm

Kindler, A. L. (2002). *Survey of the states' limited English proficient students & available educational programs and services 1999–2000 summary report*. Washington, DC: U.S. Department of Education

[On-line]. Available: www.ncela.gwu.edu/pubs/seareports/99–00/
sea9900.pdf

Knowles, M. S. (1980). *The modern practice of adult education: From
pedagogy to andragogy* (Rev. ed.). Chicago: Association Press.

Knowles, M. S., & Associates. (1984). *Andragogy in action: Applying
modern principles of adult learning.* San Francisco: Jossey-Bass.

Krashen, S. D. (1982). *Principles and practice in second language acquisition.* Oxford: Pergamon Press.

Krashen, S. D., & Terrell, T. D. (1983). *The natural approach.* San
Francisco: Alemany Press.

Kruidenier, J. (2002). *Research-based principles for adult basic education: Reading instruction.* Washington, DC: National Institute for
Literacy.

LaForge, P. (1971). Community language learning: A pilot study. *Language Learning, 21,* 45–61.

Larsen-Freeman, D. (2000). *Techniques and principles in language
teaching* (2nd ed.). New York: Oxford University Press.

Larsen-Freeman, D., & Long, M. H. (1991). *An introduction to second
language acquisition research.* New York: Longman.

Laubach Literacy Action. (2001). *A year's work in literacy: 2000–
2001 statistical report.* Syracuse, NY: Laubach Literacy Action
[On-line]. Available: www.laubach.org/USProgram/2000–01Stat/
2000–2001StatReport.pdf

Leki, I. (1992). *Understanding ESL writers: A guide for teachers.* Portsmouth, NH: Heineman.

Lozanov, G. (1979). *Suggestology and outlines of suggestopedy.* New
York: Gordon and Breach Science Publishers.

Marshall, B. (2002). *Preparing for success: A guide for teaching adult
English language learners.* Washington, DC & McHenry, IL: Center
for Applied Linguistics and Delta Systems, Inc.

McKay, S. L., & Wong, S.-L. C. (1996). Multiple discourses, multiple
identities: Investment and agency in second-language learning among
Chinese adolescent immigrant students. *Harvard Educational Review, 66*(3), 577–608.

Mun Wah, L. (Director). (1995). *The color of fear* [Video]. (Available
from Stir Fry Seminars & Consulting, 2311 8th St., Berkeley, CA
94710)

Nash, A., Cason, A., Rhum, M., McGrail, L., & Gomez-Sanford, R.
(1992). *Talking shop: A curriculum sourcebook for participatory
adult ESL.* McHenry, IL: Center for Applied Linguistics and Delta
Systems.

National Board for Professional Teaching Standards. (1998). *English as a new language standards (for teachers of students ages 3–18+)*. Arlington, VA: Author.

National Center for Education Statistics. (1998). *Adult participation in English-as-a-Second-Language (ESL) classes* [On-line]. Available: nces.ed.gov/pubs98/98036.html

National Center for ESL Literacy Education. (2003). *Adult English language instruction in the 21st century*. Washington, DC: Center for Applied Linguistics.

National Clearinghouse for ESL Literacy Education. (1998). *Research agenda for adult ESL*. Washington, DC: Center for Applied Linguistics [On-line]. Available: www.cal.org/ncle/agenda/

National Commission on Excellence in Education. (1983). *A nation at risk: The imperative for educational reform*. Washington, DC: U.S. Department of Education [On-line]. Available: www.ed.gov/pubs/NatAtRisk/

National Education Goals Panel. (1993). *The National Education Goals report: Building a nation of learners, 1993*. Washington, DC: U.S. Government Printing Office [On-line]. Available: www.negp.gov/page1–5.htm

National Reading Panel. (2000). *Teaching children to read: An evidence-based assessment of the scientific research literature on reading and its implications for reading instruction*. Washington, DC: National Institutes of Health [On-line]. Available: www.nichd.nih.gov/publications/nrppubskey.cfm

National Reporting System for Adult Education (NRS). (2001). *Measures and methods for the National Reporting System for Adult Education: Implementation guidelines*. Washington, DC: U.S. Department of Education, Office of Vocational and Adult Education, Division of Adult Education and Literacy [On-line]. Available: www.air-dc.org/nrs/implement.pdf

Nunan, D. (1988). *The learner-centered curriculum*. Cambridge, UK: Cambridge University Press.

Office of Refugee Resettlement (DHHS). (1985). *Competency-based mainstream English language training project (MELT) resource package*. Washington, DC: Author. (ERIC Document Reproduction Service No. ED264384)

Ogami, N. (Director). (1987). *Cold water* [Video]. (Available from Intercultural Press, 374 US Route One, PO Box 700, Yarmouth, ME 04096)

Oller, J. W., Jr., & Jonz, J. (1994). *Cloze and coherence*. London and Toronto: Associated University Presses.

Orem, R. A. (2001). Journal writing in adult ESL: Improving practice through reflective writing. In L. M. English & M. A. Gillen (Eds.), *Promoting journal writing in adult education*. New Directions for Adult and Continuing Education, no. 90. San Francisco: Jossey-Bass, 69–77.

Peirce, B. N. (1995). Social identity, investment, and language learning. *TESOL Quarterly, 29*(1), 9–31.

Peters, W. (Producer/Director). (1985). *A class divided* [Video]. (Available from PBS Video, P.O. Box 751089, Charlotte, NC 28275)

Peyton, J. K., & Reed, L. (1990). *Dialogue journal writing with non-native English speakers: A handbook for teachers*. Alexandria, VA: TESOL, Inc.

Prewitt, K. (Winter 2002). Demography, diversity, and democracy: The 2000 census story. *The Brookings Review, 20*(1), 6–9.

Pusch, M. (Ed.). (1979). *Multicultural education: A cross-cultural training approach*. Chicago, IL: Intercultural Network.

Quigley, B. A. (1997). *Rethinking literacy education: The critical need for practice-based change*. San Francisco: Jossey-Bass.

Raimes, A. (1983). *Techniques in teaching writing*. New York: Oxford University Press.

Richards, J. C. (2001). *Curriculum development in language teaching*. New York: Cambridge University Press.

Richards, J. C., & Rodgers, T. S. (2001). *Approaches and methods in language teaching* (2nd ed.). Cambridge: Cambridge University Press.

Rigg, P., & Kazemek, F. E. (1993). Whole language in adult literacy education. In J. A. Crandall & J. K. Peyton (Eds.), *Approaches to adult ESL literacy instruction*. McHenry, IL & Washington, DC: Delta Systems & Center for Applied Linguistics.

Rye, J. (1982). *Cloze procedure and the teaching of reading*. London: Heinemann Educational Books.

Savage, L. (1993). Literacy through a competency-based educational approach. In J. A. Crandall & J. K. Peyton (Eds.), *Approaches to adult ESL literacy instruction*. McHenry, IL & Washington, DC: Delta Systems & Center for Applied Linguistics.

Siegel, T., & Johnston, K. (Producers). (1988). *Blue collar and Buddha* [Video]. (Available from National Asian American Telecommunications Associates, 145 Ninth St., Suite 350, San Francisco, CA 94103)

Smith, F. (1971). *Understanding reading: A psycholinguistic analysis of reading and learning to read*. New York: Holt, Rinehart and Winston.

Smoke, T. (Ed.). (1998). *Adult ESL: Politics, pedagogy, and participation in classroom and community programs.* Mahwah, NJ: Lawrence Erlbaum Associates.

Snow, C. E., Burns, S. M., & Griffin, P. (Eds.). (1998). *Preventing reading difficulties in young children.* Washington, DC: National Academy Press.

Spener, D. (1993). The Freirian approach to adult literacy education. In J. A. Crandall & J. K. Peyton (Eds.), *Approaches to adult ESL literacy instruction.* McHenry, IL & Washington, DC: Delta Systems & Center for Applied Linguistics.

Spener, D. (Ed.). (1994). *Adult biliteracy in the United States.* McHenry, IL & Washington, DC: Delta Systems & Center for Applied Linguistics.

Sperling, D. (1997). *The Internet guide for English language teachers.* Upper Saddle River, NJ: Prentice Hall Regents.

Sperling, D. (1998). *Dave Sperling's Internet guide* (2nd ed.). Upper Saddle River, NJ: Prentice Hall Regents.

Stauffer, R. G. (1965). A language experience approach. In J. A. Kerfoot (Ed.), *First grade reading programs: Perspectives in reading,* No. 5, 86-118. Newark, DE: International Reading Association.

Stein, S. (1995). *Equipped for the future: A customer-driven vision for adult literacy and lifelong learning.* Washington, DC: National Institute for Literacy [On-line]. Available: www.nifl.gov/lincs/collections/eff/archive/content.htm

Stein, S. (2000). *Equipped for the future content standards: What adults need to know and be able to do in the 21st century.* Washington, DC: National Institute for Literacy [On-line]. Available: www.nifl.gov/lincs/collections/eff/standards_guide.pdf

Stevick, E. W. (1980). *Teaching languages: A way and ways.* Rowley, MA: Newbury House.

Stevick, E. W. (1998). *Working with teaching methods: What's at stake?* Boston: Heinle & Heinle Publishers.

Sticht, T. G., & Armstrong, W. B. (1994). *Adult literacy in the United States: A compendium of quantitative data and interpretive comments* [On-line]. Available: www.nald.ca/fulltext/adlitUS

Taylor, W. L. (1953). Cloze procedure: A new tool for measuring readability. *Journalism Quarterly, 30,* 415–433.

Teachers of English to Speakers of Other Languages, Inc. (TESOL). (2003). *Standards for adult education ESL programs.* Alexandria, VA: Author.

Thiagarajan, S., & Steinwachs, B. (1990). *Barnga: A simulation game on cultural clashes.* Yarmouth, ME: Intercultural Press, Inc.

Thomas, W. P., & Collier, V. P. (2002). *A national study of school effectiveness for language minority students long-term academic achievement.* Washington, DC: Center for Applied Linguistics.

Tolbert, M. (2001). *English literacy and civics education for adult learners.* Special Policy Update. Washington, DC: National Institute for Literacy [On-line]. Available: www.nifl.gov/nifl/policy/esl.pdf

Ullman, C. (1997). *Social identity and the adult ESL classroom.* ERIC Digest EDO-LE-98-01 [On-line]. Available: www.cal.org/ncle/digests/socident.htm

U.S. Department of Education (2003). *A blueprint for preparing America's future: The adult basic and literacy education act of 2003: Summary of major provisions.* Washington, DC: Author [On-line]. Available: www.ed.gov/policy/adulted/leg/aeblueprint2.doc

Valentine, T. (1990). *What motivates non-English-speaking adults to participate in the federal English-as-a-Second-Language program* (Research on Adult Basic Education No. 2). Washington, DC: U.S. Department of Education.

Van Duzer, C. H., & Berdan, R. (2000). Perspectives on assessment in adult ESOL instruction. In J. Comings, B. Garner, & C. Smith (Eds.), *Annual review of adult learning and literacy (Vol. 1).* San Francisco: Jossey-Bass.

Vella, J. (1994). *Learning to listen, learning to teach: The power of dialogue in educating adults.* San Francisco: Jossey-Bass.

Vygotsky, L. (1986). *Thought and language.* Cambridge, MA: MIT Press.

Wallerstein, N. (1983). *Language and culture in conflict: Problem-posing in the ESL classroom.* Reading, MA: Addison-Wesley.

Weinstein-Shr, G., & Quintero, E. (Eds.). (1995). *Immigrant learners and their families: Literacy to connect the generations.* McHenry, IL & Washington, DC: Delta Systems & Center for Applied Linguistics.

Whorf, B. L. (1956). Science and linguistics. In J. B. Carroll (Ed.), *Language, thought, and reality: Selected writings of Benjamin Lee Whorf.* New York: The Massachusetts Institute of Technology and John Wiley & Sons.

Widdowson, H. G. (1978). *Teaching language as communication.* Oxford: Oxford University Press.

Wrigley, H. S., & Guth, G. J. A. (1992). *Bringing literacy to life: Issues and options in adult ESL literacy.* San Diego, CA: Dominie Press.

INDEX